Psychology

Defend Yourself Against Psychological Manipulation

(The Psychological Tactics They Use to Manipulate and Deceive You)

Willie McKinney

Published By **Regina Loviusher**

Willie McKinney

Psychology: Defend Yourself Against Psychological Manipulation (The Psychological Tactics They Use to Manipulate and Deceive You)

ISBN 978-1-998901-39-5

No part of this guidebook shall be reproduced in any form without permission in writing from the publisher except in the case of brief quotations embodied in critical articles or reviews.

Legal & Disclaimer

The information contained in this ebook is not designed to replace or take the place of any form of medicine or professional medical advice. The information in this ebook has been provided for educational & entertainment purposes only.

The information contained in this book has been compiled from sources deemed reliable, and it is accurate to the best of the Author's knowledge; however, the Author cannot guarantee its accuracy and validity and cannot be held liable for any errors or omissions. Changes are periodically made to this book. You must consult your doctor or get professional medical advice before using any of the suggested remedies, techniques, or information in this book.

Upon using the information contained in this book, you agree to hold harmless the Author from and against any damages, costs, and expenses, including any legal fees potentially resulting from the application of any of the information provided by this guide. This disclaimer applies to any damages or injury caused by the use and application, whether directly or indirectly, of any advice or information presented, whether for breach of contract, tort, negligence, personal injury, criminal intent, or under any other cause of action.

You agree to accept all risks of using the information presented inside this book. You need to consult a professional medical practitioner in order to ensure you are both able and healthy enough to participate in this program.

Table of Contents

Chapter 1: What Is Dark Psychology?

What is darkish psychology, and the manner does it play a function in our lives? Dark psychology is the have a study of behaviors that coerce, have an impact on, and manipulate wonderful people (agencies or individuals) for non-public advantage. It is a phenomenon that describes the mental nature, behavior and strategies within the again of, and the manner to use them efficiently to persuade and control others. Dark psychology is nicely documented in excessive scenes consisting of criminal activity and mass manipulation in excessive manage organizations (in faith, enterprise organization, and politics). These techniques are hired in regular conditions inclusive of in income, and in conditions where diffused gestures and thoroughly determined on words can extend a deeper influence, which gives a bonus in getting what you need. Within the location of darkish psychology, many strategies and strategies efficaciously deliver human beings the better hand.

1

Understanding the Basics of Dark Psychology and its History in Research

Psychology has continually been a fascinating vicinity of check extending plenty of years, and different kinds of technological know-how and philosophy. In modern-day years, the study of dark psychology have become of growing hobby and assessment. Many developments are associated with dark psychology. These behaviors are attributed to positive types of humans and personalities who're more apt to govern. They use diverse techniques that consist of the usage of diffused, persuasive techniques or more potent strategies of manage to achieve control, private and romantic relationships, and particular connections with humans wherein there may be the capability to benefit more power. The take a look at of darkish psychology has centered on numerous man or woman kinds and professions, wherein the usage of the ones strategies is more everyday:

?   Narcissism and sociopathy are regularly related to darkish psychology due to the truth humans with those personalities use appeal, a revel in of importance over others (superiority), and the want to be adored and, or determined as a purpose to manipulate others. Their loss of empathy and incapacity to revel in regret gives them a complete range of system to advantage control within the maximum immoderate techniques in extra expert people, which may be completed subtly and punctiliously through the years. The techniques used by sociopaths and narcissists are often unethical, as they will often pass past the strategies used by specific human beings and feature the ability to cause more damage.

? In politics, campaigns and speeches rent influential language and emotion that captive humans. Persuasive techniques can regularly power human beings to vote for one candidate or celebration over a few different. Politicians and candidates are frequently pinnacle at convincing humans that they will fulfill their guarantees if elected, which may be a effective way to control their preference on whether to help them or not.

3

? Motivational audio tool are professional at the usage of dark psychology to captivate and heighten their goal market's emotional response and willpower. They have a extremely good impact on conduct and motion, at the identical time as it may additionally sell products which incorporates books and products featured at the event as well. They have a manner of creating human beings feel as even though they are capable of gain some thing, and this creates a feel-particular mind-set in which human beings are extra open to guidelines to boom and enlarge that enjoy.

? A successful profits accomplice convinces a capacity purchaser or patron in their need to buy or put money into a products or services. They may additionally additionally moreover use motivational abilties in their strategies, and in some times, evoke an emotional attachment or promise of better securing their future.

? Lawyers are professional at triumphing their instances thru the use of mental procedures to get the results in their opt for. This may be mainly effective at the same time as the percentages aren't on their aspect, despite the fact that they may shift the findings to assist their consumer.

The strategies of darkish psychology satisfy an time table every deliberately thru discovered out and advanced mind. These can be implemented as accidental strategies that we may also have picked up in adolescents from our parents and circle of relatives participants, or at paintings, college, or in our instant community. Aside from those who healthy into the companies above, anybody willing to collect their time desk via darkish psychology can increase and use those powerful skills. You may apprehend a person in my opinion that uses dark intellectual strategies to get what they need. They can be a success at it, or maybe if they're now not commonly able to accumulate the entirety, they are generally regarded for their skills for getting what they need. These humans can be the source of envy due to the fact they're charismatic and without problem convince almost everyone to agree.

How Did the Study of Dark Psychology Begin?

The examine of psychology is captivating and has been for hundreds of years. The have a have a look at of the mind dates to ancient instances on the equal time as philosophers and crucial thinkers took an interest in how we count on, behave, and characteristic. As era and our understanding of the mind improved, unique areas of research have grow to be of hobby, collectively with the study of problems associated with mind, mood and notion, and hundreds of different methods wherein we behave and reply primarily based mostly on our genetics and upbringing. Dark psychology commenced out to conform within the overdue 1800s, with the introduction of experimental psychology. Wilhelm Wundt, a scientist in Germany, modified into one of the first documented researchers of contemporary psychology, which additionally includes the evaluation of philosophy and the way we characteristic in various environments and conditions.

Wundt presupposed to observe and file numerous sensations and mind in a way that connected our sensory and the mechanics of our brain. He determined how superb chemical materials had been released and advanced or decreased in a few unspecified time within the destiny of top notch activities or incidents. Studies and their findings have become the framework for mapping the thoughts and helping more human beings to apprehend the way we assume and understand. During his profession, Wilhelm Wundt educated nearly hundred students to have a look at psychology and artwork on furthering his studies for in addition knowledge. While Wundt is considered the founder of psychology, his paintings set a popular that maintains in recent times, together with a greater specialised take a look at into experimental and cognitive studies.

Where does darkish psychology element into the look at of the thoughts? Specific regions of study protected crook psychology and other trends noticed in positive individuals, together with human beings with "darker" man or woman traits, together with a lack of empathy and a bent to manipulate. Dr. Robert Hare modified into diagnosed for his contribution to this captivating place of have a look at, which

7

turned into known as "odd psychology." He superior severa criteria and checks to decide the danger of someone with psychopathy and comparable man or woman problems or dispositions. While these studies focused at the dark factor of the human mind, it is exciting to phrase that on the same time as a small a part of the populace fits the criteria (about 3-5%), most humans, sooner or later in life, have diagnosed with the darker facet or developments of humanity, despite the fact that momentarily. Not everybody possesses the functionality of committing an unthinkable crime or dropping all empathy in the path of first rate humans. The darker issue of the mind can occupy a piece of our questioning, even inside the slightest techniques, which can be undetectable. Consider some of the following examples that we're able to revel in at any given time, irrespective of having no signs and symptoms of psychopathy or special persona sickness:

? A lack of regret is a not unusual trait in psychopaths. Most humans experience empathy and sense regret after they do some difficulty wrong, especially if it impacts someone else negatively. While empathy can range over time, it's far missing in humans with an antisocial disease. Consider, for example, at the same time as a few factor lousy takes vicinity to someone you deem deserving of the motion. You may not experience the same revel in of sadness or compassion for them. Consider if you had a hand in contributing to their downfall, although it have become justified, you can experience a sense of pleasure or view the stop cease result as a form of justice or karma. For a few humans, this turns into exaggerated while they may be now not able to feeling regret or empathy, at the least now not to the diploma due to the fact the average character. While maximum people enjoy for others, there may be conditions in which this will range, relying at the situations and our involvement.

? Manipulation and persuasion are associated with darker personalities, which incorporates narcissism and psychopathy. In the maximum excessive cases, those developments are the foundation of a "dark" persona. However, for optimum humans, developing the functionality of persuasion, and to some extent, manipulation, can be of gain and ensure their survival internal severa factors of lifestyles, such as their non-public and expert livelihood. When we discover ways to use what we understand to our gain is a human trait this is practiced via most human beings, in spite of the truth that practiced to the detriment of someone else. How you sharpen your capabilities and beautify your possibilities is based upon on how a ways you are inclined to go, and properly, you increase those dispositions.

? Charm and air of thriller are trends which are moreover associated with those who can with out troubles manipulate and convince special people. While the ones attributes do no longer robotically label a person as a psychopath or similar developments, they're without trouble used to draw particular people who are taken into consideration as conniving or sneaky as they could convince people into situations that they could in any other case refuse. A amazing and outgoing persona can healthy all people, and a few people are greater nice and receptive in first rate situations than others. People who are manifestly more fascinating can entice a crowd and come to be famous more with out problems. This approach works properly in the commercial enterprise business enterprise international and politics, despite the fact that it can be applied in small corporations or to benefit desire with own family, friends, and buddies.

These examples of tendencies are shared with the aid of many human beings, no longer virtually the small a part of the populace who're considered psychopathic or display symptoms and symptoms of narcissism, despite the fact that these developments are typically strong and extra successfully utilized by them. By understanding darkish psychology, there may be thousands to enjoy the types of methods to use in greater realistic situations wherein a nudge of persuasion or a dose of appeal can give you the gain. Despite the negativity related to the darkish aspect of the mind, there are beneficial gadget and abilities that you may use to enhance your life in lots of techniques, from art work and community to home and circle of relatives.

Chapter 2: How to Begin Implementing

Dark Psychology Techniques

Applying darkish psychology can also appear to require hundreds of test and commentary to drag off. While in greater complex or concerning situations, more competencies and exercising is critical to robust what you want, there are an awful lot much less difficult modes of persuasion that work well below quite a few each day conditions that plenty people deal with. We have all been in situations in which we want to take fee to prevent someone from taking manage. It may be tough to control the individual(s) worried, even though the occasions surrounding the scenario can be modified, sometimes fast, to shift course. Consider an incident wherein a colleague or purchaser grows indignant in response to what someone else says. The different person continues to inflate the friction by using arguing further, seeking to prove they're proper or superior. While this could enhance into a far worse level of struggle, a 3rd man or woman or celebration can calm the situation through creating a diffused but validating statement.

This can act as a "referee" 2nd a few of the 2 special events and quell any further debate. While this isn't an instance of darkish psychology or manipulation, you could start via making a peaceful, nonchalant comment to divert interest from a potentially explosive scenario; the problem come to be brief quieted and managed. This technique effectively "manipulates" the final results to a few problem more applicable.

Using clean, effective methods to govern a state of affairs involves easy psychology. It's a amazing place to begin at the same time as mastering the basics of darkish psychology and the way it may be just proper for you. The following strategies don't require lots strive, notwithstanding the reality that they may substantially form your surroundings and bend conditions to your select and come up with the benefit in some unspecified time inside the future.

1. Smile and wave at the same time as you spot a person you apprehend or have seen before, even in case you don't understand them well.

This will deliver them a notable impact, if anything, which you are best and approachable. This works preferably in art work environments wherein there are numerous personnel, together with organization offices or homes. By making your mark this manner, your amazing mind-set will stand out, and you could simply run into this individual at a conference or paintings-related occasion which can beautify your networking and career-building functionality. This method also works wonders if you are new to a selected network or network and want to make a extremely good first have an impact on without approaching too strong or pushy.

2. It's crucial to word that a few human beings are clean to engage with once you get to understand them. This includes bashful or shy human beings. Once they enjoy comfortable with a nice character or enterprise enterprise, they may open extra approximately their mind and specific extra. When you're making eye touch and make the effort to pay interest someone, even as nodding to verify and validate what they're announcing, this builds a

stronger connection to an man or woman. Building a rapport will work to your choose later on the equal time as you need them in your issue.

three. Listening to song which you experience, certainly earlier than a assembly or occasion that you preference to attend, can encourage, and prepare you to speak and behave with stronger self assurance and a sense of reason. Music is powerful and might uplift and help your reason. This interest correctly "pumps" your thoughts-set to a degree in that you feel stronger and extra able to addressing a crowd or a state of affairs which could make you worried first of all. Some public audio device or performers improve their electricity with music, motivational phrases, or affirmations for the same effect.

4. Keep positivity about you and one-of-a-kind humans ordinary. This method will prevent you from developing a horrible recognition in art work and social circles. Avoid gossip, however the reality that it seems benign or harmless. Talking approximately awesome humans

regularly results in pronouncing a few aspect unflattering behind their backs. Once this information travels, it's hard to undo, even though it become a misconception. Keeping drama out of your life is right. This definitely method that a few human beings do not need to talk with you if they will be gossip-centric, even though you can advantage more pick with one in every of a type people who are ambitious and prefer to behave in choice to talk approximately it. Also, don't say too much approximately yourself, until you don't mind it being repeated to others.

5. Keep in mind which you don't generally must reply. If a person makes an offensive or impolite observation, you have were given had been given the choice to disregard it. When you reply, you supply them the eye, and the outcome is normally an escalation to a few thing worse. When you forget about approximately them, despite the reality that this is hard to do, the onus falls on them. This is a easy however powerful way to keep away from struggle at the equal time as forcing the

alternative man or woman to be held liable for what they may be pronouncing.

6. Humor is a remarkable manner to break the ice, and it can moreover loosen any tension or bring down someone's guard. When you are making someone chuckle, they'll be a good buy a great deal less probably to benefit the better stop you, and this offers you the gain of turning the tables speedy. Laughter is exciting, so humans generally have a tendency now not to mind, but it furthermore makes them willing and susceptible to the opportunity person's intentions.

7. When you are in a scenario in which you are speaking to a person who will become too emotional, you may divert hobby by way of the use of manner of bringing up data regarding numbers or dates. In a few conditions, you could ask them a query approximately a particular huge range, cope with, or date is the answer, and it is able to "pull" them out in their emotional kingdom, even supposing in brief. This technique can be applied in situations wherein human beings experience a worrying

event. In this example, they may need to answer important questions right away regarding a crime or certainly one of a type vital event. Often, they will forget approximately important facts later, despite the truth that they may be capable of preserve in thoughts a license plate or particular emblem on a blouse proper now after an incident.

8. Use reward to offer human beings a feel of credit score rating score, although it's some thing minor, collectively with asking a question. We will be inclined to be essential of ourselves, and regularly avoid asking a particular inquiry because it seems ridiculous. When we acquire validation that the question is good, or can offer more perception into a subject, that is reassuring and gives you a higher platform to connect with them and gather a rapport.

Many of the above techniques can be acquainted to you, each due to the reality you've used them before or have skilled someone making use of them while appealing with you. Chances are, you've had someone validate a query you asked at a seminar or conference, to make you experience less awkward or inhibited about the inquiry. When someone praises you for some component, something from style to an accomplishment, it feels best. Experiencing the above conditions locations us in a position of trust, at the least in element, just so we are extra apt to concentrate and follow what the opportunity person dreams us to pay interest. It's a tactic that you can use in response, to gain the same in move lower back, or provoke at some stage in a conversation or preliminary interaction. The following techniques also are of advantage and often used to benefit receive as right with and self assurance in a person, so they'll offer a gain or service for your desire. Some of those strategies can also moreover come smooth to you, whilst others also can require a bit of exercise:

1. When you pose a query, every now and then the solution you obtain is, "what?" It may be off-setting because it seems as although the opportunity character didn't listen what you said, and you'll be eager to copy it. When this takes region, it's miles much more likely that

the opportunity character hasn't processed the question absolutely, nor have they been given enough time to soak up the records and reply in any other manner. By allowing them that small location of time, you will appear much less indignant, and the alternative character will feel happy to "hold in thoughts" the inquiry on their personal.

2. When directing an inquiry to a fixed of people, awareness on one man or woman at a time. The institution may be collectively responsible, despite the truth that they will generally delegate internal to as a minimum one or human beings to cope with each undertaking or duty internal a larger assignment. Paying interest to which people provide diverse facts on specific additives of a assignment or challenge can come up with a sturdy feel of which individual(s) are taking up sure gadgets. Once you follow this technique and determine which character to direct your remark or question, it'll supply the organisation the revel in that you are aware and paying hobby. This preference will go away a high-quality first have an effect on this is first-rate

and builds self perception in what you recognize and the way you have interaction. This tactic is specifically beneficial in business enterprise and in some unspecified time in the future of assignment interviews with a panel or company.

3. People will deliver us an excuse after they're no longer interested in a proposal, whether or not or not it's business enterprise or private. It may be clean to take one path or the alternative by way of the usage of responding with "that's suitable sufficient" to verify their lack of hobby or to hold with a rebuttal, which may additionally moreover additionally bring about reconsideration. While the primary reaction does not anything to similarly your case, a rebuttal is not continuously beneficial every. This can deter the person clearly. The third choice is to live silent for some seconds or longer, a great manner to often prompt the alternative man or woman to give an reason for their reasons for pronouncing "no." If their excuse is fabricated or untrue, they will ultimately talk themselves into a nook and lose self guarantee of their reaction. You need to

have a 2nd threat to offer once more, and with greater self warranty than the opportunity character.

four. When you encounter a person with an opposite view who desires to argue they'll be correct, it can be clean to say your opinion or factor of view over theirs to gain greater credibility. This situation has the alternative effect, and most effective reasons the alternative character to feel more vindicated or reassured that they may be accurate. Instead, technique the response with the useful useful resource of validating what they are saying first, even in case you do no longer agree or discover their opinion offensive. You can united states of america that "I see why you may expect this manner, because of the truth..." or "You have a legitimate element, and I recognize that. Here is why I enjoy that..." Not exceptional will the opposite man or woman allow their protect down a hint and no longer sense so protecting, but they may additionally take a 2nd to pay hobby for your thing of view, although you can't truly persuade them they're incorrect or wrong.

5. One of the trickiest techniques to advantage records from a person or a enterprise commercial enterprise organisation, when they're not everyday nor obliged to offer it, is to avoid indistinct questions like "who's the manager?" or "can you provide me the mobile phone variety for ___?" This situation will permit the alternative character to provide an reason for that they cannot offer in addition records because of confidentiality. Instead, ask a specific question like "Is Dan nevertheless the supervisor right here?" or "I actually have ____'s vintage cell phone variety, can you inform me if it's accurate?" This is a brief sleight-of-hand that may disable the alternative person's sense of protective the facts, and they'll permit their guard down, wondering you can in my opinion apprehend the character or item that you're inquiring approximately.

6. The company enterprise is hard, and it could make human interaction complex while the patron or patron isn't always cooperative. Clients may be mainly tough when they should look ahead to a services or products. When this takes place, we're often inclined to make an

apology and kingdom, "sorry for retaining you prepared" or "I apologize for the put off." While many corporations require their personnel to reply that they may be sorry and take the onus for a industrial enterprise' shortfall, it's far greater powerful to answer with "thank you to your patience," as this casually recommendations for his or her response to fall regular with displaying forgiveness and persistence. Often, the reaction can be "that's suitable enough, it's not your fault" or "I apprehend you're busy, take the time.

Chapter 3: The Principles of Dark Psychology

What are the thoughts of darkish psychology? Dark psychology targets to rent useful gear and strategies to manipulate, manage, or persuade different human beings to gain a bonus. This area of check strives to apprehend and determine what mind-set human beings have and the manner they located the ones strategies into motion to manipulate others. Understanding the requirements of psychology is a high-quality advantage in lifestyles because it enables us understand the human state of affairs and the manner we use psychology to prey or target others for our gain. In a few instances, it's instinctual, whilst different kinds of manipulation are in fundamental terms intentional with an time table or precise very last effects. Dark psychology has been in comparison to criminal hobby and psychopathic reasons, despite the fact that many humans use numerous varieties of those techniques to regular what they need in life.

Dark psychology embodies more than the far forestall of the spectrum that we regularly see depicted in movies approximately serial killers and sociopaths. This refers to a class of mechanisms which can be performed via many humans to accumulate what they want. Dark psychology additionally includes manipulating conditions and/or humans in their direction to success. While styles of emotional and intellectual abuse are associated with manipulation, many subtle yet impactful techniques can provide you with a higher hazard of having what you need, often with the opposite character ignorant of what's taking region. There are many additives of darkish psychology that spark controversy about how certain techniques are used and their impact on exclusive humans; however, there is a pleasant element to using a few processes in instances in which you could beautify your chances of achievement. This ebook will display you the manner to apply factors of dark psychology for your advantage, in every subtle and realistic techniques. These techniques, even as completed efficiently, decrease the danger of failure on the equal time as growing the benefits of achieving your purpose or cause correctly.

Why Is Dark Psychology Effective and Why Do People Use It?

The strategies of dark psychology are powerful. They can exert undue have an impact on over many people, which include a few parents which can be commonly resistant to manipulate or persuasion. People use dark psychology for plenty motives. They growth and use diverse strategies and techniques to obtain goals, every for ulterior motives and for broader gains for different human beings or businesses as properly. Persuasion is implemented for many outcomes, which include getting the following selling, securing a task, or gaining pick out interior a social circle. Money, relationships, and improving social repute are most of the most common motives for using darkish psychology.

Dating, Sex, and Relationships

Charm and aura are factors used to influence someone to interact in sex or begin a dating short, regularly without the assure of willpower. This issue isn't complex wherein each events accomplishing intimacy have the identical desires and are open about their intentions, whether there can be a long-time period dedication or not. Self-hobby and instant gratification are on the coronary heart of using persuasion, and in a few cases, greater strong office work for manipulation, to persuade someone to date or get involved romantically. There are many reasons why persuasion is useful on the start of a relationship and a manner to have interaction in intimacy:

? Enjoying sex without self-control is exciting and offers immediate gratification to the person who succeeds in seducing a person they may be interested by. In a few times, the concept of getting intercourse is the most effective reason, and proper chemistry isn't wanted.

? Do you recognize the concept of pursuing someone, of chasing each one-of-a-kind character until they provide in for your seduction? Seducing a person is a thrill or rush for a few people, particularly if it consequences in mutual appeal. Sometimes the chase is more interesting for superb human beings, and the exhilaration falters once they get what (or who) they need.

?   Securing a date and operating in the course of a relationship with blessings, every sexual, social, or each, may be each different reason to rent darkish psychology techniques. Even in times in which the alternative individual feels a spark of enchantment, it's no longer usually enough to steady courting and the possibility of a dating without persuasion.

Doting on someone, giving compliments, and provoking them to have a communique with you may be finished in every subtle and extra direct techniques. In a few times, a extra candid technique works , and in different situations, a gentler way brings fulfillment. You can benefit masses from a courting, which could bring about better financial safety, connections to social circles, and enhancing or putting in a popularity interior that organization and past. Self-interest is the cause in all instances, regardless of the reality that there is easy interest given to the possibility man or woman at instances. Using dark psychology to seduce a person will typically advantage the as soon as pursuing that the most effective they need.

Why do human beings pursue relationships with darkish psychology strategies? The reasons variety drastically from the selection for sex and straight away gratification to pursing particular kinks and fetishes while others aim to secure a romantic courting for the long term to regular economic benefit or decorate their reputation. Persuasion is commonly the remarkable technique to use while pursuing a person, as you'll need to ensure there is a risk they're inquisitive about the identical. There is also a level of transparency, which gives the alternative individual a demonstration of your intentions, even in case you select out no longer to reveal the entirety certainly. For instance, someone searching out intercourse without dedication may be instantly-forward about it, despite the fact that they'll not expose their preference to discover kinks and fetishes till they'll be concerned with you in element.

Whether to disclose an excessive amount of or too little inside the starting must make a large effect at the final consequences of a situation, due to the fact not anybody will want to comprehend too much, or too little will go away them trying to understand greater. For this cause, many human beings will awareness on precise websites or groups that cater to their precise needs and goals, and at the equal time as persuasion also can though be used, they may have a higher hazard of getting what (and who) they need.

Dark Psychology in Politics

During campaigns and spherical election time, the prevalence of the use of manipulative and persuasive strategies are regularly used. Candidates use emotionally charged speeches and concentrated on their combatants negatively as part of a technique to win. This can get up in any respect tiers of presidency, from metropolis or town councils to huge positions at a country or federal level. An elected respectable or flesh presser will use similar techniques of their feature, in order that they hold their recognition and solid future fulfillment. Voters are intently precipitated via candidates in brilliant ways, despite the fact that essentially the very last consequences or purpose is the equal: they need to win, and the more votes and useful aid, the better. What techniques convince citizens to aid one candidate over some different, and what techniques art work?

? Taking credit score score and highlighting beyond triumphs and successes is a sturdy manner to start, as it builds self belief within the target market, and might attraction to uncertain human beings. Claiming non-public credit score rating for situations whilst topics are generally transferring in a nice route and moving the blame of any poorly orchestrated options or mind at the opposing activities or applicants is some different tactic used often. Sponsored commercials and supporters of 1 celebration or every different regularly leap on board to claim their allegiance and make use of persuasive techniques of their personal to advantage attention for his or her personal business or notoriety while helping a particular baby-kisser or celebration on the equal time.

? Some politicians are expert public audio machine and apprehend how to body or together institution the popularity quo as something greater super than it's far. This takes area once they strong a role within the place of job, and at the way, they'll usually convince you that they're the answer to any problems that could rise up. They may go as some distance as accountable warring parties for being negative and/or incompetent. This may be effective whilst there are crucial worldwide sports in motion, and surely anybody is searching out some issue or someone accountable. It's an opportunistic time for applicants and politicians to position themselves as part of the solution and take credit score rating for any progress, whether or not or not or not tremendous or small, to decorate their recognition and credibility.

Many humans may think they might see via political reasons and hints, and but most of the identical humans will pick out the same (or similar) applicants, however signs and signs and symptoms and signs and symptoms and signs that there may be a manipulative nature at play. This is due to the reality political personalities attraction to a big target market and regularly assemble their systems on what people need the most while giving them a experience of desire if they will be elected. Political strategies additionally have a look at at paintings and in community networks, wherein specific human beings use their reputation to propel themselves into positions of electricity and recognition.

Corporate and Business Strategies in Persuasion

Sales and the advertising of a company' products and services align with persuasion and manipulation, often on a extra unconscious degree. Most people who artwork in marketing or sales are aware about how promotional advertisements and campaigns purpose to cause precise humans or demographics. This may be seen within the very nature of classified ads, and promotional campaigns, and the way it works frequently is going unnoticed. When we take a higher, extra scrutinizing have a observe how advertising and marketing and advertising works, we however may not see each super detail used to sway our mind to buy and use a products or services. Some strategies are diffused, at the same time as others are greater overt and obvious, and but we're induced every way.

In industrial corporation, the persuasion and manipulation are frequently implemented in positions of immoderate strain and authority, whether it's a CEO making drastic restructuring changes to a organization and want to influence the alternative Directors to agree, or a profits partner searching for to maximise their fee. In many conditions, persuasion is a catalyst that makes an impossible state of affairs indoors reach. Strategies in industrial enterprise require pretty some conversation, frequently to personnel, customers, and/or stakeholders who may be worrying about the future in their business enterprise or line of company. Dark psychology frequently works its magic inner those plans of movement. These strategies require progressive "massaging" of phrases and the capability to narrate to humans on a human diploma, whilst simultaneously eliminating some issue from them to be able to advantage you. The industrial enterprise global is brutal on this manner due to the fact the bottom line continuously takes precedence over the whole thing and all and sundry else.

Forming Alliances in Business and Personal Situations

One of the most important steps in beginning a brand new process or becoming a member of a employer is making an outstanding affect and analyzing who you may be given as true with and paintings with without difficulty whilst keeping off hard people and conditions along the way. If you begin an get entry to-degree assignment in a huge enterprise agency, the capacity to climb the ladder to a better, extra profitable role may furthermore look like a stretch, until you comprehend a way to community and stick out from your friends. One of the maximum important elements of constructing a remarkable community at your area of employment, or interior a modern day network or upon joining an corporation corporation is to discern out clean attributes about the human beings you'll art work and socialize with:

? Who is straightforward to talk to and communicate with, and who isn't approachable? You'll take a look at that the very first-class human beings to talk to can offer hundreds of records about the organization and may even will can help you in on some secrets in the event that they opt for you.

? When meeting in a collection, it may be hard to decide which people like every considered one of a type, specially if they all behave cordial and professional notwithstanding their variations. When this takes place, be aware of human beings after they talk, and phrase who they have a study when they explicit themselves. It is human nature to have a study someone who we generally like and accept as true with. This is mainly the case even as a robust declaration is made, as the person supplying will searching for visible confirmation from their "supporters" for a nod or display of approval as they talk.

? Follow their gaze and word who they look towards, as this may provide you with a exquisite idea of which humans are inside the same group or on the identical "facet."

? When you're making a announcement or present to the same institution, popularity at the identical humans with whom you apprehend (or strongly suspect) can be given as actual with you and help your path. It is a powerful way to collect an alliance with people you may no longer but apprehend due to the fact they're able to assist give you the tools desired for the mission and might gain from it themselves. This is likewise a diffused act of persuasion.

? If someone else has a excellent idea, but they do now not commonly want to express it, take at the process for them. It may be a high-quality way to provide their idea advantage and get a few credit rating for assisting them in the way. If you mention your idea originated from someone else, this will help offer you with more popularity for retaining it. This is specifically possibly if you're accustomed to dealing with an business enterprise or leader who doesn't attention on man or woman ideas however may additionally take a collective brainstorm or referenced concept notably.

? When you cope with a terrible state of affairs, de-escalating may be a tough project. If you're taking the least confrontational approach, this could make it an lousy lot much less complicated to treatment. Imagine discovering someone within the manner of stealing a few objects from artwork, and you are the manager and can be held liable for their actions. Instead of threatening them with disciplinary movement right away, even though this can be forthcoming, you may be in a safer situation to advocate them that there are cameras and movement sensors that could choose up on what they're doing. This takes the onus off you and makes them responsible. When the motion need to be stated, they may no longer always hold you accountable, and manage will commend you on handling the scenario properly.

Allying is not the difficult mission it is able to seem like and can be performed the usage of easy, smooth-to-have a look at behavior that would direct humans to technique you greater often, particularly if you are inclined to speak new ideas and take phrase of different people's moves. Being observant is one of the maximum important components of achievement and might make you stand out whilst you can don't forget or have a study some thing that others push aside. As you emerge as familiar with greater human beings at paintings and the way they behave with every one-of-a-kind, you'll have a better experience of the way to speak with them and shape strong connections that may provide you with a clearer course to what you need to gather.

Ask for What you Want and Make it Count

What takes vicinity on the equal time as we want a marketing and advertising or enhance at artwork? We frequently cover within the decrease again of smaller requests that could lead us in that path finally. When this happens, we pass over out on the whole advantage.

Consider a situation in which you want to ask for a enhance, after walking within the identical function for over 365 days. Your time-honored overall performance evaluations are satisfactory, and you're aware that the possibility of a pay boost or vending is an opportunity, however now not a assure. In this example, many personnel forestall brief of asking for a enhance and instead ask if there are each different positions or room to address extra responsibilities, hoping this may mechanically translate into a merchandising and, or growth in pay. Often, this outcomes in taking up more responsibilities and no longer the usage of a real boom in the future. Not remarkable is this nerve-racking to tackle extra paintings with the equal pay, but it furthermore makes a few different declaration in your corporation: that you are willing to do greater for less, and they will preserve to take gain of you for it.

Go huge when you ask what you need at art work. If you need a specific final consequences, ask if the query you are prepared to pose will carry it approximately, or if it's simply a distraction from what you can have now. There are a few reasons why we don't boldly ask for what we in reality need, along facet the subsequent:

? We count on that what we in reality need is out of the question and that we received't get it. This state of affairs takes area because of the reality some employers offer their personnel the have an impact on that they need to be happy approximately their undertaking, mainly at the same time as the economic system is sluggish. Inadvertently, this offers employees the concept that they need to be glad to art work and no longer pursue any similarly pay or promotional options until a miles later time.

? Be direct and don't revel in ashamed to invite for what you need, although it seems trivial. Sometimes a small decide on granted can hint toward some thing a exceptional deal more large in a while. You might also need to installation that you'll get a touch of what you want now in education for huge ambition within the future.

Chapter 4: Strategies for Manipulation in Advertising

Consider some of the reasons we're apt to be privy to a few classified ads more than others, and the strategies which have an impact on us. It isn't any mistake that positive jingles or slogans ring in our minds for a extended period, even as certain photos are branded into our reminiscence to continuously remind us of a specific eating place, brand, or product. Among all of the effective strategies used for advertising, the exceptional are subliminal because of the reality they wake up our subconsciousness and make a long-lasting effect. By the time we recognize how effective or memorable an ad is, we've already been impacted through using it extended within the past. Consider the following techniques that now not most effective convince you to buy a products or services. The subsequent time you word a billboard or banner in the direction of your television or computer show show, recollect some of the subsequent attributes and the way they effect and hook up with you on a private diploma:

? The placement of objects or photos is an over-seemed approach that works to govern our mind into processing what we've a observe in a certainly one of a kind manner. For instance, placing an image at the left facet of a display show or advertisement will boom the fluency or pace at which we way, often resulting in a super response or have an effect on. How regularly are we able to take a look at the placement of items on a display display or billboard? It likely in no manner crosses our mind, and but it has a unconscious impact on how well we accumulate the general message.

? Placing gadgets on the left-factor and from positive angles can also produce a more favorable have an effect on of the object itself and the message. If the advert features a specific products or services on this way, you're greater interested by it definitely. Some research imply that including someone or unique devices are held or getting used, the favorable impact of putting the item at the left is lots less powerful.

?   When you add a utensil or device to a few other item, to show off its use is rate, this placement and state of software makes an effect. Generally, human beings need to look a product in a state wherein they are able to relate to the usage of it, which include butter on a slice of bread, instead of displaying a loaf of bread in a bag or placing a spoon or fork in a mouth-watering bowl of soup or cereal. Shoes, garb, and add-ons are high-quality tested with their laces or openings (zippers, buttons) obvious, so that they appear practical and realistic. In those types of instances, human beings can relate to the use of these products and might be greater apt to shop for them.

?   The duration of lettering or textual content has a profound effect on how humans recognize an advert or message. Studies completed on actually developing the scale of phrases and messages confirmed a proper away impact at the emotional response of the audience. Generally, the larger the font or lettering, the greater impactful the message. This impact is magnified when a particular phrase or phrase in a sentence is bolded or enlarged more than the very last words or letters. This is a effective manner to rouse an emotional response and is frequently applied in fundraising or reputation campaigns, however moreover within the advertising and advertising and marketing of products, regularly to align them with providing a gain to meet an emotional want or desire.

? When high priced services or products are promoted, sturdy and assertive language is fine for a success persuasion. Those individuals who are attracted to brilliant offerings, and merchandise associated with the texture of importance and urgency, to attempt the subsequent and most up to date made from pleasure. For most commercials, the idea of the usage of a greater aggressive tone is prevented because of the truth humans usually do not like feeling as if you're attempting to steer them, subsequently the unconscious and diffused approaches which might be regularly used. For high priced or specialised offerings that appeal to a more hedonistic or pride-attempting to find target market, this is an exception.

?   Using similar phrases or rhyming, even the use of a small or short poem, may additionally have a fine effect on human beings. When a slogan is balked at as stupid or juvenile, it despite the fact that grabs humans's hobby, and it remains with them, notwithstanding the initial bad reaction. Slogans and jingles that rhyme or have a catchy set of terms that sound similar are difficult to overlook. You can also moreover keep in mind unique advertisements and commercials from your adolescents definitely because of a particular line or phrase that became unique. This is the genius behind advertising and its effects in both the short and lengthy-term. Consider the following examples:

• "Do you need some detail greater? Shop at our shop!"

• "You deserve the first-rate. Shop with us, we'll cope with the relaxation."

?   As formerly stated, photographs at the left aspect of an ad have the effect of being processed rapid and greater undoubtedly, although if an photo is massive and complex, it is able to paintings fine placed at the right aspect. This is because of how our brain tactics visuals. If you place your product at the left, the logo can be greater powerful at the proper.

? The period of your product or brand makes a distinction, and it will increase the persuasion component. You can convince ability customers to attempt your logo with out overtly saying it. In some times, it's far recommended that lowering the size of the product is first-rate if it's miles given a middle diploma or highlighted on a web page or ad with a border or photos. Generally, growing the dimensions of a product is top-high-quality for purchasing the eye you want for advertising.

? In addition to the font duration and lettering, the color and design make an effect as nicely. Other attributes that still go away an effect consist of spacing, the web site of the letters, and the street or font fashion. If you need to show off your logo as fancy or decorative, you could want to use a cursive font, despite the fact that this can no longer attraction to the attention if they are hard to test or combination in with the ancient beyond or image. For impact, lettering need to be like a label: it must stand out and range sufficient in shade and style to be visible without issue.

? Ads or campaigns that promote splendor and nicely being merchandise regularly use angular designs and prolonged, slim strains and strokes in their font. This offers the concept of beauty due to the fact those patterns are easy to study and taken into attention visually terrific. Placing devices or photos on the left aspect of an advert has the advantage of being processed speedy and visible as favorable and beautiful at the equal time. Thin lines in font, despite the fact that a modern fashion is used, make a better have an impact on than a thick, bolded fashion.

? Designing a completely unique brand or fashion of writing is a few different way to hook up with human beings, as they'll normally consider your products or provider when they spot your brand or any related fashion. From children, plenty folks can remember at least one restaurant or keep from an vintage brand, even though it's been out of movement for decades. Product designing follows the same precept. Color coordination and lettering goes an extended way to securing a familiarity and planting a business enterprise effect for your thoughts in case you want to final for months, years, or probably an entire life.

? Color is impactful for plenty motives. In company, many humans positioned on unique sun shades or patterns to hold a sense of authority or, no less than, to get your interest and hold you engaged. This works in advertising and advertising and marketing thru giving the target audience a sense of urgency: crimson and yellow are generally used for classified ads that say "save you" or "warning" before introducing you to a brand new home protection tool or safety device. The cautionary approach appeals to many human beings whilst they are concerned approximately their safety and safety. Cooler shades collectively with blue and inexperienced are first-rate for advertisements that supply a carrier that is supposed to calm or soothe, while crimson, orange, or yellow come up with a more enjoy of urgency to behave to clear up your issues right away. As effective as color may be in advertising and marketing, it is able to litter or blur the overall message, which can be counter-effective. In these advertisements, handiest part of the message, usually the wording and one or gadgets inside the photo stand out as superb or colourful, while the the relaxation of the ad is pastel or diminished.

? People or version placement in commercials create the face of the product, and regularly with a incredible response or smile. This impact offers the target market a first rate impact of the usefulness of the emblem and its appearance.

One most essential feature of marketing is to make an appeal to a particular demographic and evoke an emotional reaction. We may not continuously word how we react to an ad until later at the same time as it creeps into our mind about a personal enjoy or feeling. This impact can be added approximately later in next marketing campaigns, in particular while a fine logo or product has staying energy and continues to foster a relationship with us.

Traditional products will often rebrand and re-bundle deal deal to appeal to a converting generation. A slogan or message may be delivered to a products or services to align a business enterprise or brand in help of contemporary-day occasions and movements inside the news. This has the impact of gaining new customers and may create a strong and powerful emotional attachment. Some human beings will join their loyalty to a selected brand or enterprise because of their political stance or moral practices. A brand or corporation that doesn't adapt to cutting-edge conditions turns into an "endangered species" in organization and risks loss as a result.

Framing is an powerful device that takes a awful or immoderate quality state of affairs, together with a clinical condition or common inconvenience, and markets an answer in the form of a products or services. Pharmaceutical commercials are infamous for selling a choice to almost any clinical problem. They should observe strict recommendations for advertising and marketing and advertising and marketing, including the disclosure of aspect results, even though feature own family-pleasant topics that align with our choice to feel consolation and comfort from ache, regularly because of many continual fitness conditions they promote treatment for. Negative framing refers to the usage of a challenge or worry we've approximately life, whether or not or not it's a virus or a problem about growing crime in a network, to market safety merchandise or shielding device to provide us a feel of improved safety. When framing is horrific, it is most probable to create an urgent want to react short, it is frequently the case and can reason a excessive amount of success inside a brief time. This is powerful at the same time as finished in a time-sensitive manner to cope with present day activities and troubles of in recent times.

Positive framing is a manner to generate interest and hobby in a product that you can in no way undergo in mind in advance than. When a trouble is posed and an answer provided, the excessive amazing frame conjures satisfaction approximately a brand new services or products with statements which encompass "see what we are capable of do to beautify your fulfillment nowadays" or "beautify your stamina and thoughts health with our innovative emblem…" Even the maximum skeptical reader will take a higher appearance to find out greater approximately the amusing or fashion. This method is a slight, however powerful manner to seize each person's hobby and convince them to peek, if now not outright buy your product.

Inclusivity is a chief topic of communique in lots of factors and is regularly involved in lots of discussions from socioeconomic to political subjects. Advertising has also picked up at the significance of showcasing kind of their commercials and slogans, and as many agencies shift their interest on which encompass more samples of society, at the side of fashions with "real" body sorts and people from each age, backgrounds, and ethnicities, the target marketplace constantly expands and engages more people nowadays. Gone are the instances of conventional roles from a long term within the beyond. Advertising is openly greater inclusive with photographs and the manner merchandise as soon as marketed to at the least one organization are in reality branded for all and sundry, from motors and private pc structures to beauty products. Featuring "real humans" in classified ads has had a excessive effect on improving the way human beings enjoy about the products in the ones advertisements, giving the advertiser or corporation the benefit.

Chapter 5: What Methods Applied in Dark Psychology

There are smooth however powerful techniques which can be used to benefit desire and control in a unmarried-on-one conversations, that could evolve into more complicated systems of commentary and understanding which people to "intention" or interest immediately to hire those techniques. Some specific strategies and practices are herbal for a few human beings to increase on their very non-public, even as others will workout and educate their behavior to turn out to be more powerful of their capacity to steer and gain electricity.

The Basic Concept of NLP or Neuro-Linguistic Programming

Neuro-linguistic programming or NLP is a exercising this is utilized by many professions that entails declaration of bodily and verbal cues in special people and using techniques to recognize and have an impact on them. NLP has been utilized in lots of professions due to the truth that its development nearly half of of a century in the beyond, and on the identical time because it's been the supply of controversy and debate on its effectiveness, the practices are nonetheless extensively used these days. More details on the particular techniques and the way they're used are featured in chapters 4 and five.

Hypnosis

A effective and regularly neglected method, the practice of hypnosis grew in reputation within the 1700s and has regularly grow to be more not unusual in its use ever for the cause that. Hypnosis is defined as a workout that regulates popularity in a manner which could manage, and in some instances, supersede positive types of behavior and notion. Despite arguments within the route of its use or effectiveness, hypnosis is used in recent times to deal with many situations which include addiction, trauma, and behavior manipulate. It's considerably finished for masses of reasons and treatments, lots of which people discover beneficial in lifestyles. Therapists will conduct hypnosis to recognize underlying motives deep indoors their patients, which frequently encompass resurfacing past reviews, at the side of traumatic events.

How effective is hypnosis? Some humans are greater open to perception and effect than others, which means that that the effects variety. The extra influential the man or woman, the more likely you may be capable of set off a country of hypnosis and exert extra control over their thoughts and moves. In this us of a, the thoughts is effects persuaded with plenty less try than in our normal conscious u . S . A .. You can instruct someone to undergo in thoughts painful or difficult memories greater and now not the use of a problem on this u.S.A. Of the us, as a way to apprehend their emotions and mind sooner or later of the technique. These techniques are frequently utilized in therapy, despite the fact that there are special instances while hypnosis is used, collectively with live level performances, in which individuals of the intention marketplace volunteer to be induced right into a country of hypnosis for enjoyment capabilities.

One of the maximum debatable aspects of hypnosis has constantly been its purpose and the manner it is carried out. In medical research and for recovery reasons, it is able to provide a window into the thoughts for similarly understanding of tactics our mind and cognitive procedure works. Some research have indicated an improvement in reminiscence at the identical time as hypnoanalysis is applied, although there were critiques of fake or distorted memories that have had a stressful impact on people. When used within the context of entertainment for marvel rate or as a way to gain energy or manipulate over a few different individual without their information, it could be a subject of debate as to whether or no longer it should be used the least bit.

When is hypnosis used to persuade and guide someone towards a positive choice or to meet an ulterior motive? The power of this exercise is in the palms of the character inducing the kingdom of their goal, whether it's to relieve them of a scientific state of affairs or intellectual trauma or to bring about a country wherein they will use their strength to influence and "trick" the alternative man or woman to look and behave otherwise. Hypnosis is greater than controlling what the opportunity human beings see and remember; it can regulate their present day notion, conduct, and may be used as a tool to mildew their actions. The strategies utilized in hypnosis are often diffused, but powerful, just like the subliminal messages we see, however won't overtly word, in mag, tv, or on-line classified ads.

How Hypnosis Works

To set off a country of hypnosis, a licensed hypnotist will use numerous cues or suggestions to shift your hobby into a trace. This may be carried out with the repetition of terms or sounds that progressively bring about this nation. Once this is completed, the affected character or one-of-a-kind character tales a having a pipe dream-like united states. They may additionally experience as though they'll be in a dream and not sincerely aware. Hypnosis works like NLP as it shifts a person into an altered country of reputation by using the usage of verbal cues at the side of repetition. Certain forms of music or regular rhythms have been seemed to result in similar states of numerous consciousness, which may be often visible as euphoric or "excessive." During this nation, a person is more likely to look at instructions and focus on an object or idea, even as in a regular country of recognition, they may commonly overlook about or disregard it. This characteristic offers the hypnotist the advantage due to the truth they now can use hints to awaken first-rate moves and behaviors that would otherwise no longer be feasible.

Inducing an Altered State of Consciousness for Greater Influence and Persuasion

How can you use hypnosis on your gain? You don't ought to be an authorized hypnotist to take advantage of the techniques used in this technique. Often, we are subjected to versions of hypnotic impacts or may additionally additionally furthermore take a look at a person else's shield is allow down, and they may be greater receptive to pointers or thoughts at the same time as they may be underneath the affect of alcohol or specific materials that loosen their inhibitions. This country may be brought approximately via different method in numerous settings. Consider the following conditions and the way they could modify a person's potential to fall under a greater suggestive or agreeable united states:

? A live live performance or song event with loud, rhythmic, and repetitive beats can bring about a trance-like country in a few human beings, wherein they're much more likely to provide in to someone and let their guard down. Have you ever approached someone at a club or venue and discovered them far greater agreeable and perceptive to you than at work or in a few other place without the equal stimuli? This may be because of being below the have an effect on of alcohol as nicely, although the rhythmic nature of track could have a hypnotic effect on a few people.

? Meditation and some varieties of yoga have been used to gain a outstanding level of hobby. Some human beings find out they're extra receptive at the same time as they'll be in a meditative kingdom. Self-hypnosis is each different way wherein people can activate a greater suggestive kingdom inside themselves, which can also impact others round them if done in a collection putting. This will have a profound effect on influencing a couple of person at a time.

? Certain pills or hallucinogens can activate numerous states in which you are aware and targeted, however moreover much more likely to bend to someone else's pointers and plenty less hesitant in favored.

? Some web sites or tv shows also can characteristic a segment with shifting gadgets or drift or design, rotating with consistency that brings approximately a hypnotic kingdom or trance. This isn't continuously considerable, and might best final momentarily, even though it is also a not unusual device used in marketing and advertising or gaming apps to preserve gamers and clients engaged for hours at a time.

While there are many apparent strategies wherein we may be swayed to shop for a services or products or have a look at a fashion or commercial enterprise agency, there are numerous subtle processes that we be aware each day, from the patterns or hues applied in classified ads on billboards to banners that rhythmically dance across your laptop show display inside the middle of an internet verbal exchange or whilst playing a workout. When requested how a lot we see in advertising and are encouraged each day, we probable nice recall a fragment from our attention, on the identical time as our subconscious keeps a long way extra, and has a sturdy impact on our spending and manner of lifestyles choices, irrespective of questioning that our options are truly our personal.

Chapter 6: Learning How to Use Techniques of Persuasion and Manipulation

Understanding the severa trends of darkish psychology can provide you with a bonus in lots of conditions. Taking a take a look at out each of these dispositions will provide you with a better concept of what it manner to be persuasive as opposed to manipulative, and how a dose of air of mystery and paying nearer interest to the following individual you meet can take you a bargain further than anticipated.

The Difference Between Persuasion and Manipulation

Many humans use those terms interchangeably, despite the fact that they're as a substitute one-of-a-type in their definition and purpose. The technique or technique used relies upon at the specific state of affairs and the activities of the character. Persuasion is often regarded as a gentler shape of manipulation that focuses and builds on the overall intention of some other man or woman. The desire to steer a person else may be a way to encourage them to pursue or accomplish a assignment that they will be considering, despite the fact that they may revel in dubious approximately their abilties or the very last consequences. In this manner, you're applying strain or encouragement to consistent their choice in a specific direction. They are already thinking about this as an preference, and the act of persuasion will provide them the desired "push." Manipulation, however, conceals your actual reason and goals to steer the opposite character that there can be a gain for them (or collectively) whilst the end result is a bonus to you. This calls for stronger strategies, which growth with severity whilst the alternative man or woman is evidence towards locating out to your pick out. In reviewing the variations among persuasion and manipulation, it's clean how every tactic has its benefits in particular situations.

Persuasion

? There is transparency inside the technique of persuasion, without a hidden time desk or deceit, because both activities are aware about the choice to sway the opposite individual in the path of a desire.

? The one of a kind man or woman is considering the muse and genuinely hasn't finalized their selection yet. This may be a together useful go together with the flow if they stand to advantage in some manner from the persuasion, and all they want is that greater cause or affirmation to hold.

? Persuasion may be a selfless act at the same time as the other individual stands to gain more than in reality everybody else. For instance, you may convince a person to use for employment in a modern employer, notwithstanding the truth that they don't sense they're licensed, in spite of the truth that also can strive if they're satisfied that their resume and credentials are virtually without a doubt really worth attention.

Manipulation

? The act of manipulation requires concealing your real intentions to sway the alternative character's mind proper into a desire for you to provide extra of a benefit for you than them.

This need to endorse taking someone into making an steeply-priced buy to gain your earnings fee, even if it is clean that this is not the most viable preference for them.

? There is very little transparency in manipulation. There is usually a hidden time table just so the alternative character isn't continually aware about their loss of advantage and what you stand to benefit from it. Even after they turn out to be privy to this, similarly manipulation, if skillfully accomplished, can convince them enough that there can be some issue in it for them.

? Conjuring a experience of urgency or worry and the usage of emotional expressions can bypass an prolonged way to persuade someone to determine that they'll in any other case in no manner undergo in mind.

Both manipulation and persuasion have the same goal, despite the fact that the underlying methods and reasons for the usage of both techniques range considerably. The diploma to that you use persuasion is predicated upon in your unique situation, and whether or not manipulation is wanted to take a more potent technique toward securing what you need. For example, final a sale also can start with a persuasive technique, as you convince the functionality customer that they want the product. When they do not want, you can growth the strain by using manner of way of noting there may be a sale that ends inside an afternoon or that the product(s) will best be available for a restrained time, and not making the acquisition will forfeit any future benefits. Sometimes this tactic, as harsh as it is able to appear, can effectively "push" someone to signal a agreement instant, to keep away from lacking the sale, or spend extra than they to begin with anticipated.

Understanding the Importance of Developing Good Persuasion Skills

The most skillful manipulators start as masters in the artwork of persuasion. They have superior the competencies to have a observe and decide the opportunity man or woman (their supposed aim) and what it's going to take to influence them to decide or pass in a particular course. Persuasion is an powerful set of competencies which could assist every body from enterprise employer leaders and CEOs to everyday situations going for walks in retail or earnings positions. It's an vital set of strategies to apply for your private lifestyles whilst handling indecisive human beings or hard scenes that want a person with the capability to nudge and direct an person or group of humans within the right route. You can also moreover already use persuasion competencies in lifestyles with out statistics it, as it's far a exercise lots oldsters look at in early life, collectively with convincing a determine to shop for ice cream or visit the neighborhood park or fairgrounds. It's a addiction masses folks have found at a extra youthful age, even though as we grow old, we adapt our communique into adulthood. Further improvement of persuasion techniques can be completed by means of manner of the usage of the usage of what we have already got even as making use of new strategies that art work properly in masses of conditions.

What Are Your Strengths? Use Them to Your Advantage

Are you right analyzing humans or finding some issue in not unusual with a coworker or new acquaintance? You can be an superb verbal exchange starter or apprehend the proper time to say particular phrases or phrases while they may have their preferred impact. All those attributes and more have to make your persuasion very powerful and a success.

Point of View from Another Perspective

One of the devices missing in hundreds of attempts to influence or persuade someone isn't being capable of see their element of view. This is the myopic or quick-sighted view and might dismantle any chance you've got in convincing a person. It not most effective limits your potential to make a massive reference to the alternative man or woman, but it's going to also increase the possibilities that they'll see you as rigid and lacking compassion till you may exhibit an appreciation or records in their issue or factor of view. Making this connection bridges pretty some gaps that many human beings have, even though do no longer frequently see a chunk-round while searching out to reconcile, then make their case. Persuasion will become far more effective when the alternative character is happy that you understand and famend them.

Expect Arguments and Prepare for Them

Some persuasive strategies are not acquired without a struggle, and because of this, you need to plan for the hazard which you'll come upon resistance. Most human beings aren't as indecisive as they'll seem, and any try to sway their opinion or choice in some distinct route can be met with a combat. Consider this a opportunity for all situations and prepare what you may say in reaction to them. A counter-argument ought to be finished respectfully, and paying attention to the alternative person, in spite of the way a good deal you can disagree or dislike what they have got to say, is important for framing your subsequent glide and the way you can continue.

Become a Problem Solver

This calls for correct listening abilties and determining which limitations the alternative individual has that may save you them from being satisfied. For example, if a person doesn't have the cash to start a small investment fund or make little contributions each month, you can offer a loose assessment of their rate variety for thoughts. This can assist them "find" a manner to in shape a weekly or monthly contribution to make. Instead of explaining all of your motives to persuade or persuade someone first, allow them to us of a their reviews and issues. Not handiest will this make your interest easier in persuading them which product or alternative is tremendous for them, but you'll truly have a more captivated audience due to the truth you listened and stated them first.

There is Always Common Ground

We regularly see each first-rate's versions before we percentage what we've in not unusual with others. This frequently results in misunderstanding and using phrases or phrases that may not connect with others. For instance, if you discover that some different person enjoys live theatre, you can relate to them via asking about their preferred productions, then drawing them right proper into a conversation to influence. If the unique object that you have in common with them relates to part of the persuasion or choice you desire to sway them within the direction of, then you definately definately in reality are at a exceptional gain.

Show Confidence and Don't Be Afraid to Show It

Many folks who aren't too tough to influence also can end up deterred if they see a touch of hesitation or uncertainty to your tone of voice or body language. Being confident in what you have to mention and what you need to convince them to do is a wonderful step in the direction of securing success. People experience self warranty. For this cause, exercising your speech and what you want to mention, and make sure your voice is assertive and robust. The more practice, the lots much less complicated it is going to be to make an impactful effect that instills self assure inside the extraordinary individual.

Using Body Language That "Mirrors" the Other Person

This approach may additionally appear subtle, but its impact is powerful in appealing to exceptional humans. Mirroring is used whilst you phrase a shift in frame weight or moderate gesturing or posture changes that you have a look at in someone, then duplicate them in a way that isn't too obvious. If someone is speaking in a easy tone and is slight in their speech, it's far powerful to bring your tone of voice into the identical realm, as this could deliver them the have an effect on that you are meeting them on the identical degree. A stronger tone or voice or more blunt method can be required if it's far used and predicted by means of the alternative man or woman, even though attain this cautiously, and take a look at whether it's far having a nice effect on connecting with them. Mirroring gives the opportunity character the have an effect on that you are following their lead and allowing them to manage the direction of the communique, even as you effectively practice persuasion techniques.

Make Notes and Remember Key Information

Taking notes at some point of a verbal exchange, in particular in business enterprise or expert conditions, may additionally appear unusual if you are not used to this exercising. Taking notes is a top notch concept for some motives:

? You don't should do not forget each element of the conversation, and making notes will capture the maximum vital points that you may talk over with later, at the equal time as within the equal conversation or at a later time.

? Taking notes shows interest in what the possibility man or woman has to say. They will take a look at this as a effective and may reveal extra statistics as a end result, information they will be heard and recorded.

? This will build confidence inside the special man or woman, and they will keep in mind that you could use this facts to recommend or offer beneficial information.

Learn and Use People's Names

When a person hears their name, they not most effective enjoy the customised contact of the communication, but recognize which you do not forget who they're, and are much more likely to answer favorably. Using their name in a verbal exchange more than as quickly as, no matter the fact that no longer excessively, is a manner to allow them to understand that you are thinking about them for my part, which has a pleasing response.

Never Give Up and Be Persistent

Persistence pays off, even though it's some distance often avoided or disregarded as too aggressive of an approach or unlikely to paintings. On the opposite, cautiously timed and regular persistence in following up with people should make a prime impact on how possibly they may be to trade their minds or finalize a choice. This is in particular critical in situations wherein the opportunity individual is not positive what to determine and asks for time to expect it over. This is a high chance to obtain out to them. Take into consideration any connection you made on your preliminary meeting and use this on your benefit to stable a operating courting with them. Your touch with them may be the catalyst that secures their choice for your need.

Research Ahead and Prepare

Know your goal and purpose with precision. This can great be completed at the same time as you recognize what you're speakme approximately and get to apprehend who you are speakme to. The more you recognize the individual and their desires, the more you can appeal to them in this diploma. They will pay attention to you more closely and on a personal degree in case you attraction to them on a deeper degree. For instance, if someone owns a small business organisation or is employed in a selected project of work, this can come up with the benefit of connecting with them. You can also use this records to persuade them that a particular products or services is proper for them.

The Basics of Manipulation and How it Compares and Evolves From Persuasion

Manipulation is a miles more potent form of persuasion that targets to get you what you want, no matter the final results of the opportunity individual. When you are making the shift from using persuasive techniques to greater manipulative approaches, there are some key factors to keep in thoughts. Persuasion is regularly the primary manner to persuade other human beings, specially if the challenge includes "pushing" or convincing them to move or preserve in a particular route or selection. Manipulation is a stronger method that requires extra control over the other individual, that is often completed at the same time as the alternative person is on path toward shifting inside the contrary path of in that you need them to go. At this thing, you'll want stronger strategies to exchange their thoughts. You'll need to steer them with more effective methods, that might result in making them experience a feel of obligation or strength of will to you or an commercial organisation organization, that would "guilt" them into running in your pick out or the usage of fear or a sense of responsibility to regular the equal result.

When do you cross the road from persuasion to manipulation, and how can this be finished effectively?

? It's essential to recognise the opportunity person, their desires, and their dreams. They may additionally additionally say "no," and while this could be their genuine reaction, take note of hesitation and whether or not they may be nonetheless wondering internally, even though they seem precise of their choice. This can leave a mild beginning of possibility to influence them to mention "yes" with factors and mind that would attraction to them.

? Convincing a person which you understand what they need, even better than they do, can take some exercise and expertise. In this way, you play the professional, and with self perception and know-how, this may be pulled off. It is a shape of manipulation that offers them the affect that you may figure them out and understand their desires properly, even higher then they can, to benefit their self notion in you. For instance, you will be grew to emerge as down while supplying a issuer to a small commercial organization, though thru information the records and economic struggles of the enterprise, you could advantage their acquire as real with with the aid of using convincing them that what you have to provide will boom their earnings and success. Relating to them on a non-public stage and appealing to their need for advanced business enterprise can be the breaking factor that convinces them to exchange in your want.

Persuasion or Manipulation? Learning the Differences Between Them and How They Can Be Effectively Applied to Your Benefit in Various Case Scenarios

As defined in advance on this economic damage, persuasion and manipulation are comparable in some methods, with certainly one of a kind versions in how they are used to get what you want. Persuasion is the exquisite ability set on the identical time because the alternative man or woman is on their way to figuring out and desires a more potent enjoy of guidance. They need a completely last push or nudge to exchange the "perhaps" or "I expect so" to a particular "sure." Manipulation can alternate a "no" or "I don't think so" into a "yes."

How do persuasion and manipulation techniques artwork in real case conditions that we're handling each day? Often, we don't apprehend what number of opportunities there are to steer someone in our decide upon, and we are capable of miss this chance via not efficaciously searching at their conduct and planning efficaciously what to do subsequent. How does this play out in situations at work, inside the workplace or showroom, or private relationships?

Scenario 1: The Sales Associate

Sonia became employed as a profits associate for a immoderate-give up furnishings keep. The showroom became well organized to reveal a great sort of top extraordinary products at a pinnacle fee fee. During the primary week, except for some small orders, Sonia didn't close to on any massive profits. She have become given a month to expose her capability, and in the direction of this time, she decided to observe numerous strategies in every persuasion and manipulation that might skip her within the course of meeting her desires. In the second week, she met with a circle of relatives who modified into interested by a present day consuming room set. The specific set they had been considering modified into one of the most costly fashions and would be enough to set up self warranty with Sonia's boss if she made the sale.

Brenda, the spouse of Greg and mother of preteen kids, come to be keen on the prestigious consuming room set, however her husband's hesitation. He come to be worried approximately the rate range and whether or no longer or no longer they could provide you with the money for it. Brenda confident Greg they had the coins and deserved to splurge on themselves. Sonia faced a predicament: she have to stand thru and watch them decide on their private, taking a passive stance, or she may additionally want to attraction to the emotional desires of Brenda, who desired to invest in their new home. The children regarded bored and wandered spherical the shop, leaving the dad and mom to argue approximately the selection to shop for the table and chairs. During this time, Sonia had a danger to do not forget a manner to enchantment to them with the useful resource of looking at and reading the subsequent:

? They should discover the cash for the eating room set, but Greg became satisfied it was not a bargain, even as Brenda preferred to decorate the advent of their domestic. She discovered the acquisition as an investment, at the same time as he seemed it as a burden.

? Both kids have been antique sufficient to be in junior immoderate or secondary university, which supposed they probable had homework to do every week. The eating room table might provide a communal area for each kids and their parents to artwork collectively, as needed.

?   A appropriate satisfactory ingesting room desk and chairs might also remaining longer, provide a higher guarantee, and in preferred, extra fee-powerful for a family. This ought to make a higher impact on website online site visitors and extended circle of relatives, in particular over the vacations.

?   Any troubles about purchasing for the furniture unexpectedly can be without difficulty dealt with through a financing plan.

?   Both mother and father labored entire-time, even though price variety had been tight due to a few extra, surprising expenses over the last couple of months.

Sonia prepared to provide the own family an amazing financing plan with an low-value interest rate even as deferring the primary payments with out interest. They may additionally not require a down charge, and they might order the set and feature it brought inner in line with week. During the vacation season, which have become genuinely months away, having a cutting-edge eating room set might be a pleasant "gift to themselves," Sonia cautioned. The concept of treating themselves lit up Greg's face, as he determined out they were on foot so tough, and coming home to a sleek, snug seating association wherein they may experience home-cooked meals as a family changed right into a worthwhile funding. When Greg hesitated to sign the provide, Sonia in a well mannered way reminded him that he modified into doing this for his own family, and they may all thank him for it later. With that assertion, the sale changed into made, and Sonia changed into on her way to make the number one of many extra earnings within the furnishings hold.

What strategies did Sonia use to steer every Brenda and Greg to shop for the furnishings? In the start, she already had Brenda's "purchase-in," which have end up in her favor. Brenda didn't require an awful lot persuasion to buy the ingesting room set, as her thoughts modified into already made up; but, Greg become opposed to it and endorsed a miles much less high priced option as a substitute. This conflict of phrases between the couple may additionally want to have without difficulty precipitated Brenda accepting Greg's desire till Sonia stepped in to convince them to take it. Persuasion become the number one method due to the truth at the same time as Greg was leaning closer to a "no," he have become usually at the fence and willing to move in the direction of his partner's idea with a bit of convincing. If Greg became able to persuade Brenda that some other preference turn out to be higher for their family, Sonia might likely ought to use stronger, more manipulative strategies to sway their desire again in the direction of the specific eating set.

Scenario 2: Making a Date

Todd changed into charismatic and suitable searching, which emerge as an easy way to benefit choice and make a splendid effect on most humans. He changed into successful in corporation and labored in advertising, which allowed him to fulfill many new humans regularly. Most girls he encountered cherished his organisation, and his attraction received him many dates and some intimate relationships over severa years. On one occasion, Todd met

Dana, who have end up first-rate, appealing, and surely savvy in her line of organization. They met at a conference, and Dana have emerge as effects swept into a conversation with the useful aid of Todd, who changed into eager to get to understand her extra. Not handiest have become he interested in her romantically, he observed how properly people gravitated towards her, and the way this will gain him to be in her presence. Securing a dating with Dana may additionally want to signify lots to benefit, in business company and his non-public lifestyles.

After meeting for the second one time at every different business business enterprise convention, Todd entertained the concept of asking Dana on a date. He made it sound playful, now not as crucial as although they were simply grabbing dinner with the possibility of a drink. Dana hesitated before mentioning that she became unavailable. Todd nodded and smiled as even though to truely take shipping of her reaction, notwithstanding the reality that he determined to find out more approximately Dana, in case it'd assist him gain her choice and likely convince her to remember him sufficient for a date. It changed into smooth in advance than everything; Todd retrieved a enterprise organisation card from Dana and did a few digging on line into her line of hard work, which worried event planning. He observed out that she wasn't married. She became famous with masses of people and regarded to take an hobby in antiques and avenue trips, in keeping with her professional social media profile. Dana's credentials have been exceptional, and she or he appreciated to excursion extensively. This gave Todd some data for the subsequent time they might meet.

A month later, Todd met with some colleagues for lunch. He in fact selected (and advocated) a café whilst he all of sudden bumped into Dana. Todd knew there was a mild threat that Dana might be inside the place given that she had stated some close by shops and companies in quick in the route of a previous conversation. Their communique became more relaxed than common, and Todd invited her to enroll in him for coffee after lunch, which Dana with out a trouble common. During the 2 hours they spent together, Todd casually stated his entertainment of vintage shape and specially indoors décor that resembled flip-of-the-century designs. This resonated with Dana, and he knew she loved antiques, which made it smooth to find out commonplace ground. Todd additionally said that he changed into considering taking a pressure out of town to find out some small towns finally over the summer time, which piqued Dana's interest as nicely considering she turn out to be eager on avenue trips. During their alternate, Todd become cautious to test Dana's gestures and mannerisms, which indicated that she become more eager to get to comprehend him and probably follow a date. Instead of pursuing the question up to now, Todd furnished his employer card and nonchalantly asked Dana to offer him a call if she wanted to enroll in him on his avenue ride. She preferred the cardboard, and an afternoon later, she referred to as to ask greater about his power out of city. Todd acted vaguely in the beginning, which recommended Dana to provide an cause of greater of her love of excursion and antiques. Furthermore, she unleashed masses greater about her personal life and struggles, which made her a fulfillment nowadays. She might speedy be prepared to simply accept the invitation to dinner, Todd concept, and shortly thereafter, Dana agreed to fulfill for liquids and dinner at a community eating place. Their assembly speedy advanced right into a strolling dating in which Todd obtained extra information approximately Dana, and the way her facts must help him gain access to greater enterprise connections and possibilities than earlier than.

What techniques did Todd use, and had been they persuasive or manipulative? Initially, Todd appeared right away-beforehand in his technique to invite Dana on a date, and whilst he did find out her attractive, his primary cause emerge as to strong a better networking technique to in addition his time table and steady extra contracts. Dana did experience Todd and his commercial enterprise enterprise, regardless of the reality that she must no longer have considered a dating with him until finding common ground sooner or later in their coffee date. While Dana became not in opposition to relationship Todd, she can also have brushed off him clearly. When Todd professed his ardour for antique shape and format, he grow to be merely looking for a subtle way to connect with Dana, as he had researched and determined about her fascination with antiques. Todd didn't care approximately structure, nor did he locate road journeys thrilling, despite the fact that he become inclined to use the ones gadgets of interest to steer Dana that they can be a exceptional healthful, and it labored. In this example, Todd used manipulation for the subsequent motives:

? He focused on his private and expert gain from relationship Dana and did now not endure in thoughts that she could advantage from him, nor did it trouble him. Even if Dana may advantage from their courting, this modified into not a aspect in Todd's selection to seduce and pursue her.

? Todd stood more to benefit from a functionality dating, or even working friendship, with Dana. He decided on to pursue her for courting due to the truth he need to discover more about her on an intimate diploma, giving him extra blessings than his colleagues and in all likelihood securing extra industrial organisation due to her have an effect on.

? The commonplace ground among Dana and Todd have grow to be in reality fabricated, that may be a shape of deception because of the reality Todd had no real hobby in her passion for antiques and avenue journeys. By convincing Dana that they shared those hobbies in commonplace, he led her to surely take delivery of as real with that they may make the exceptional couple.

In every conditions, persuasion, and to some extent, manipulation may be used to offer the end end result you want from a person, despite the fact that they're now not apt to make that specific preference at the start. At the very least, persuasion works on folks that are heading within the same path you want them to move, via giving them that extra push or incentive to finalize their desire, that could gain both you and them. Manipulation is the following level even as persuasion fails, or virtually isn't sturdy enough to get the outcomes you want.

Developing Charisma and Charm to Influence People

The act of persuasion, manipulation, and their achievement is predicated upon carefully on how charismatic you're. Unless you attraction for your purpose or target market, you'll fail to convince every body which you have a few issue they want. This applies to nearly each scenario. Thus putting in an amazing rapport and sensing that the possibility character likes you from the start is crucial. It's the muse upon which you can assemble an entire lot greater. Charm and air of secrecy are natural dispositions for some humans, who appear to put little or no attempt into gaining select with almost certainly all and sundry. For maximum humans, even human beings with the prevailing of putting in place an splendid first have an impact on, growing the amount of aura requires preserving the alternative character or company for your pick for a prolonged period, until your motive is fulfilled and, or they make a choice or flow into to your assist.

What does it take to establish and enhance air of secrecy and enchantment at the same time as assembly a person for the number one time, and the way will you purchased this without fumbling or making simple errors? Many elements want to be in location in advance than you could execute your course of action, which incorporates in which and on the identical time as you'll meet, the apparel you located on, and the manner nicely you may maintain the other character's interest. It's vital to investigate the organization or person when you have information earlier, which includes a capability purchaser and, or candidate. If you are utilising for a interest or role, it's suitable to recognize as masses about the enterprise or employer you need to use, so you can display off your recognize-the way to electrify the interviewer.

The following attributes are crucial for growing air of mystery, as they set the degree for a fantastic script and easy, herbal drift of alternate amongst you and the opportunity character or humans:

?   Be gift and banish and preconceived mind you may have about a specific individual or what they represent at the equal time as you meet them. While it is right to hold an opinion or feeling approximately someone, any judgments you're making need to be located aside. There is always a risk that what you recognize or take a look at is wrong, which can taint your common effect. Approach the meeting or invitation with a easy, smooth slate and with an open mind.

?   Keep your awareness on the alternative man or woman. If there can be a set, attention on who is speaking, and nod, use eye contact periodically and if invited, make contributions to the communicate or communication. If you interrupt by way of using mistake, quick express regret and quickly offer the opportunity person to preserve. Give them the spotlight and validate what they're pronouncing. Once they shift the dialogue to you with a query or a request for detail, smile earlier than you start, and in case you fumble, chortle at your self and make it part of the go along with the flow. Keeping this interest will let you interrupt from anxiety, and it gives the opportunity person a chance to look your "human" side, further to being a expert.

? Avoid fidgeting or playing collectively together together with your mobile cellphone or distinct gadgets. Most parents are so related to our transportable electronics that it is able to without difficulty take our hobby from a real-time conversation. People have a tendency to view this as especially disrespectful in some circles, and some human beings will actively request that every one gadgets be have come to be off or switched to "silent" mode. Even within the absence of devices or system, fidgeting together together with your arms or touching your face, among extraordinary involved conduct, can devalue what you are saying and the because of this in the back of it. If you experience this could be a trouble, don't forget folding your hands on the table within the front of you, leaving them there at some stage in the interview. If you use your hands to gesture at some point of the conversation, pass again them to the table right now after to make certain you keep away from fidgeting. Practice at domestic inside the the front of a mirror just so this turns into easy to pull off when you are prepared.

? Sometimes a query or observation is indistinct and goals rationalization. One of the maximum not unusual mistakes humans make is to count on they apprehend what you want as an answer with out records the entire query. In some interviews or conferences, you'll be requested a question like this for this very reason: it's an brilliant possibility to check your listening skills and determine in case you apprehend what's requested of you, and, or whether or not you are assured enough to ask for clarification. If there's even the slightest doubt, usually ask the possibility man or woman to make clear. Is the question well-known and open to interpretation, or extra particular? When an trouble is accurate, providing an example this is immoderate top notch and uplifting ought to make an brilliant impact.

? Sit or stand genuinely, so you don't revel in any soreness. Don't be afraid to shift your weight from one leg to any other or trade your seat or role on a chair to enhance the manner you enjoy. Any enjoy of pain can seriously mar the way you behave or reply. You may additionally respond too quick or swiftly to avoid further discussion or nod and, or agree even as you propose to go back to the alternative. To keep away from the ones eventualities, commonly function your frame with out trouble on a chair, couch, or popularity to maximise your comfort at some point of the communication.

? Leave a space of at least 3-4 seconds earlier than responding to a query, even if you understand the exact solution that you could provide. This pause gives the interviewer or other individual that you are giving the response some immoderate idea. They will take this as a signal that you anticipate earlier than you speak, which is for your choose out. A individual who responds too rapidly or without an lousy lot training will frequently make errors and fumble or stutter, even supposing they understand the difficulty depend properly. Avoid any projection of nervousness or uncertainty via taking the ones few seconds. The interviewer will now not expect the answer proper away, like a sport display, with a restrained time body to answer. Take that short duration to installation your thoughts and take a deep breath earlier than you talk.

Charisma is all about how we provoke the opportunity person with our character and the manner we engage with them. If you have were given a humorousness or a shared interest with them, permit that become a focal point, even for simplest a minute. This technique can effectively harm the ice and supply the alternative person a not unusual floor with you, in spite of the fact that they don't recognize you but. For some human beings, a quick praise or near commentary about a person's place of job décor or fashion is welcome, as extended because it flows with the general mission count number of the interview or communique. In a greater casual placing, commenting on a person's look can be greater ideal than a agency assembly or commercial enterprise interview.

Assess every parameter for my part and decide which approach of method works tremendous, with out overdoing it or making it too visible that you're searching out to benefit someone's want.

What want to you keep away from within the direction of a meeting or conversation that could restriction your chances of success? There are many techniques to fail with the beneficial aid of best now not wondering earlier than talking or developing a remark too fast with out regard to our audience. A effective go along with the float can fast flip unpleasant with an beside the point funny story or feedback that's taken offensively. Some errors can derail a communication or interplay fast, that you need to keep away from as masses as feasible:

? When you are listening totally to respond. This exercise can be nicely-intentioned in case you want to maintain a conversation and the opportunity character enjoys speakme with you. Unfortunately, this practice manner you're now not truly taking note of what they are saying. You can effects pass over a crucial fact or observation with the resource of leaping head-first in reaction. When this occurs, it may result in pronouncing some thing irrelevant or insensitive, certainly due to the truth you didn't pay interest well sufficient.

? Avoid changing the hassle until it's crucial. There are conditions on the same time as converting the problem is appropriate, even though usually this isn't required. The trouble rely can be a supply of passion and emotion for the opportunity individual, and skipping past it could have dire effects. They can also enjoy which you don't absolutely care about what they have got to say or recognize their enter. As a give up end end result, something you're announcing after may additionally additionally have the identical effect. There is a time and location to trade the priority, as an example: in case you observe that the current-day-day hassle do not forget is annoying or triggering for the opportunity person, or if the subsequent problem is associated and for fine that they will welcome the transfer.

? Don't interrupt, due to the truth it's far a advantageous-fireside manner to lose your credibility during a communique and preference with the other character. This exercising is taken into consideration rude, and it can also be a sign which you don't have the staying electricity or timing to statement while it's far appropriate to achieve this. Children commonly generally tend to interrupt ultimately of a verbal exchange after they experience impulsive or excited about some aspect, even though this tones down over time and is averted as we end up adulthood. Hold onto any vital mind you want to percentage and wait till there may be a harm in the communique.

? Avoid distractions, as they'll be in maximum cases a state of affairs in case you are meeting on a hectic road or workplace wherein human beings are always strolling via and different sports are taking area. Focus at the man or woman in front of you and phrase them because the anchor within the route of the whole discussion. If you emerge as momentarily distracted, speedy make an apology and go back to the communique.

Examples of Using Charisma and Charm to Your Advantage

How are you able to exercise the blessings of growing air of thriller and appeal in real-existence situations? Consider the subsequent conditions and word how each person employs numerous tactics to ensure they make an tremendous first have an impact on. What we've a have a look at is terrific put into exercising as quickly as possible to make sure we've got were given an fantastic draw near of what works wonderful in numerous situations. For example, in case you plan to wait a venture interview, practice first with a pal or member of the family to get an concept of processes the drift of verbal exchange may be.

Scenario 1: The Job Interview

Samantha have become excited to attend an interview for a characteristic as assistant supervisor at a prestigious commercial and home constructing downtown in a large metropolis placing. She had all the qualifications, despite the fact that she knew there had been many extraordinary applicants with comparable credentials. Samantha preferred to make an high-quality impact and rating a strong rapport with the panel of interviewers, as this could ultimately bring about a career possibility in belongings control. To prepare for the interview, Samantha researched the control commercial enterprise corporation presently beneath agreement with the constructing, further to the facts of the vicinity, the demographics, and unique developments that might display useful. She wore professional apparel and taken a posted replica of her resume, cowl letter, and references to the interview. Samantha changed into apprehensive but furthermore confident that she possessed the right skill set for the task.

The panel interviewed a boardroom with glass walls, permitting a view to the outside. The organisation changed into busy, with a ordinary flow of people coming and going. Samantha changed into passionate about the present day décor and standing related to the employer that she nearly forgot in which the office end up located, which almost made her past due. Fortunately, she requested a person within the hall and rapid made her way into the boardroom earlier than the interview started out. Upon arriving, the whole panel of interviewers became there, ready to engage in small communicate and communication before the dependable meeting. Samantha took advantage of this possibility to speak approximately her favored sports activities agency and her love of biking outside. When the interview started out out, Samantha made certain she come to be prepared to answer questions like "Why do you need to art work for us?" and "What makes a remarkable property manager?" The interviewers sensed that Samantha become keen to pleasure others and can stumble upon worrying conditions whilst pronouncing no to a patron at a hobby internet web site. They provided some situations that featured tough-to-manipulate humans and superb practices in responding to them.

Samantha listened carefully to each situation, pausing in advance than she replied. They had been a bit greater hard to reply than anticipated, but she did her amazing to locate the right way to answer. In the second one scenario, Samantha supplied solution alternatives that she was hoping is probably correct. Towards the surrender of the interview, the panel asked Samantha if she had any questions. Despite being nicely prepared for the interview, she hadn't expected being asked this and grow to be afraid to say that she hadn't any inquiries, so she asked about the organization's statistics and improvement plans. This regarded to resonate with the organization, and she felt proper approximately the interview in full-size. Samantha changed into knowledgeable that she could achieve a call to wait a have a look at-up second interview if she grow to be considered a appropriate candidate.

Assessment of Scenario 1

Samantha did a wonderful hobby of having geared up for the interview and struck an exceptional rapport with the panel. They cherished the conversation in conjunction with her and noticed that she had a high diploma of know-how approximately the business enterprise and changed into keen to analyze extra. Samantha wasn't the most professional in property control but did offer lots of extra, transferable competencies that she included in her interview, which gave everyone a good have an impact on. When thinking about Samantha's regular presentation, how nicely did she carry out? Following the dialogue, the panel of interviewers noted Samantha's assembly and concept about whether she is probably a amazing healthy. They loved how rapid she spoke back while asked some organization-related questions with precise eventualities. In reviewing their next institution of applicants, they determined to provide Samantha every other hazard. She seemed well mannered and agreeable, which became top for constructing rapport with colleagues and clients; but, she may want to need a stronger remedy to address difficult situations at the job. The 2d interview may also need to permit her to show greater of her hassle-fixing capabilities and decide if she might be an terrific wholesome.

Scenario 2: The Development Proposal

Darren modified into interested in presenting an concept to his town council. As part of a developing organisation, he had his eyes set on constructing a brand new complex that could offer a area for shops and apartments or condominiums above. He had an formidable idea that won't resonate well with every body. A comparable perception turn out to be furnished a few years in the past with an overwhelmingly terrible response. Many of the town's citizens desired to preserve the historical price of the houses and didn't take nicely to modern dispositions, although the authentic systems remained the equal and untouched.

Before his scheduled meeting with Darren, the metropolis council had typically been divided on further proposals. They have been eager on maintaining their metropolis in its unique state, regardless of the possibilities, there can be extra tourism and possibilities for sales. Darren got here organized. He knew the objection he faced and modified into geared up to cope with it. Having lived inside the metropolis for three years, he had a spouse and children who had been actively involved within the community. They have been properly-preferred and revered. Darren would possibly use this information to his advantage and spotlight the need for the town council to test the future.

Upon assembly the council one nighttime, Darren approached the table eagerly, however not too much, certainly so he would now not appear too much like a salesperson. The reception have become quality and cordial. Half of the council have grow to be already in choose of the development, so Darren knew he needed to persuade a few greater human beings to offer it a threat. He appealed to the reality that maximum council people had households and cherished the nearby businesses in town. Since the economic downturn, the metropolis's corporation suffered, forcing at the least shops to shut and extra to downsize. Upon offering those information and evoking an emotional reaction from maximum people, he ultimately supplied his plan of development as a state-of-the-art manner to resolve the city's problems.

Almost right away after unveiling the plan and imparting the form, Darren met with competition from members. He desired to interrupt, as that they had responded with incorrect statistics approximately the task, however he constrained himself and permit them to voice their issues. Once they finished, Darren described his interest of a preceding plan and the way it wasn't received nicely. He expressed that his idea modified into in evaluation to the previous notion, which have come to be lots huge and will negatively impact the view of the metropolis and impact small businesses.

Darren defined that if the city council have end up willing to pay attention to his model or beautify the idea, that he may want to happily provide them with more records to provide them extra records on his imaginative and prescient. The council agreed to be aware about Darren, and they have been surprised to check that the scale of the venture have grow to be masses smaller than formerly imagined. There can also be communal regions inside the constructing for local artisans and commercial enterprise owners to exhibit and sell their brands.

Upon reviewing the entire plans, the council ushered a collective sigh of consolation, but they were left with some indecision. The council determined that giving the latest inspiration a have a look at, which emerge as more in determine upon of the bulk of citizens, can be honest to reconsider, due to the reality the metropolis did come upon an economic downturn, and they wanted accurate thoughts to hold more tourism. The idea didn't guarantee an stepped forward float of industrial organisation, nor did it plan to enhance travelers; but, the ability for becoming an amazing deliver of income for residents and enhancing their morale modified into a first rate purpose to reconsider.

Assessment of Scenario 2

Darren changed into properly organized and brought a number of statistics to the desk in the route of the city council's meeting. He have end up able to take a once more seat to pay attention to all people's troubles while supplying a concerned, considerate technique to the metropolis's issues at the same time as introducing a contemporary perception that become now not just like in advance than. He changed into organized to wait and understood the plight of the town council. Darren highlighted the fact that whilst he come to be a current resident, his own family changed into happy, involved in the network, and they have been there to stay. While Darren become eager to reply to pushback from the people of the council, he stored his thoughts till surely all and sundry modified into equipped and willing to pay interest. This worked efficaciously in his pick out due to the fact had he answered too brief, they could experience pushed or manipulated. Darren's persuasion worked due to the fact he appealed to the fears and issues of the people, further to the citizens of the town. He supplied practical thoughts and solutions that he had already blanketed into his plans.

After the council meeting, the individuals gave the idea greater perception and attention. Collectively, the council modified into divided, despite the fact that they did see an area for the new belief of their future. They moreover stated the way it modified into important to maintain in mind new mind for reviving their town at the identical time as retaining the statistics of their citizens. The suggestion didn't right now motive a entire agreement, even though it did shift the communique to a greater agreeable stance: to reconsider some shape of improvement, whether or not or not or not it changed into simply in line with Darren's plan or not, and to invite greater proposals to provide the town greater options to choose from. While the council meeting wasn't a complete win-win for Darren, it gave him a shot at bidding on a very closing task option, which may be reviewed for a totally last selection at a later date.

Recognizing and releasing blockages

Mental blockages are insidious little beasts that conceal inside the unconscious. Although you word that a few component is there that is slowing you down, you cannot apprehend wherein this sense comes from and why it's miles there. There is not any manner to make those insidious topics seen, neither with an ultrasound nor with a TC or an X-ray machine. This is why it is so tough for remedy and era to make intellectual blockages visible and consequently tangible.

To address and remedy a few factor intangible is a huge assignment. The small ghosts make life unnecessarily hard, rate a whole lot of power and electricity and reason pressure. These elements avert you in strengthening your self-self guarantee, gaining self-self belief, shaping your very personal existence and making your individual the priority. But there may be a way to discover and dissolve blockages.

This does now not paintings like bodily ache, in which there are unique capsules and painkillers.

In order now not to enjoy intellectual pain, people are actual regressionists.

They paint even the worst fears with colorful colors in order that they do not must appearance them in the malicious, sparkling eyes. But that is wherein the problems begin, which emerge as a massive monster, a intellectual blockade. But what are intellectual blockages? These are programs that run on your subconscious and save you you for your thinking and acting. They rise up in notable mental conditions that don't in shape into the preceding machine. They cannot be processed so without difficulty because of the truth there's an excessive amount of intellectual pain. The subconsciousness creates behavior patterns to suppress this pain and to cope with it. You should shield yourself towards this through the use of confronting this emotional ache. Grab the burdensome mission with the aid of way of way of the hair and attempt with all your electricity to allow skip and dissolve the blockages.

Because the ones malicious specters have a company grip on you and prevent you from dwelling a satisfied, fulfilled lifestyles.

Mental blockades

• you sabotage each step of the manner.

• may be the reason of severa illnesses.

• cause effective problems to recur time and time again, presenting you with the sensation of being stuck in the equal location.

• can be dissolved by way of using a brilliant mind-set.

Perhaps painful research in your youth have led you to have highbrow blockages which as a teenager furnished themselves as complexes, despair, low vanity and self-self belief. To release emotional blockages, you need to address the topic "letting skip".

Set the whole thing to restart with release

There are a number of techniques that you can use to discover ways to permit go to launch highbrow blockages. They artwork thoroughly and will convey you masses further. If it have been no longer for this one big chew that weighs you down. You can't discover a appropriate lever to launch this blockage and to reinforce yourself-self warranty. Just the right lever is the belief that you need to allow visit dissolve the mental blockage absolutely and now not to preserve any more ballast round with you. But what is supposed through letting bypass?

"Letting pass way not anything extra than announcing goodbye to fantastic terrible thinking and changing it with incredible questioning!"

You release yourself from a disturbing scenario, a terrible occasion that reasons you strain.

How does it paintings?

A small instance:

You are on the full teach on your manner to artwork and function not been given a seat. You are inside the hall with many different folks that are also on their way to paintings.

Suddenly the train using force has to make an emergency prevent. The man or woman reputation within the returned of you loses balance and pushes you as an opportunity more or tons much less in the back, so that you have hassle stopping yourself. You are full of top notch anger and rage. Why can not this individual keep on nicely to prevent this type of scenario? This awful feeling creates pressure. You turn round to offer the person a right opinion and suddenly the situation has changed truely. Because earlier than you stand a person with darkish sunglasses and a cane for the blind. He is wearing a yellow armband with 3 black dots on his arm. Immediately your feelings trade. The resentment and anger are neutralized and modified with the useful resource of know-how and compassion.

What reasons this variation in feeling?

You have received a very precise view of things because of the fact you previously misjudged the state of affairs and assumed wantonness.

The new state of affairs has allowed you to allow move of anger, resentment and stress and replace them with new emotions with out being aware of them. Your perspective has changed. To launch intellectual blockages, you want to alternate your view of the scenario or the event inflicting it. This neutralizes the pressure hormone and the blocking emotions. More splendid emotions arise.

However, it is not constantly easy to trade one's perspective and rise up new techniques of questioning because of the reality the injuries have too deep roots. It is critical that you apprehend why you react so negatively to incredible situations. Maybe the blockage has not whatever to do with outdoor influences but is based at the reality which you are to your way and can not jump over your shadow.

First try and find out the inspiration of the intellectual blockage. To try this, it's miles very vital to discover the unique tendencies of the intellectual block.

Can you discover with the subsequent factors?

• When you're addressed with the aid of using way of someone, the blush rises in your face.

• If you have got to talk within the the the front of various people, you are forced.

• During an exam you black out, despite the fact that the exam cloth indoors out.

• Do you have have been given the feeling of losing manipulate on the identical time as matters do no longer flow into the way you need them too?

• Do tormenting reminiscences and thoughts from the unconscious time and again emerge, which might be connected with the beyond?

If you recognize one or more conditions quality too nicely, you are very possibly to be emotionally blocked. It is exactly people who need to be resolved. Unfortunately, there may be no magic potion that gets rid of the internal blockades as though with the useful resource of magic. You need to emerge as energetic and face those emotions. Do no longer attempt to forget about your feelings. By figuring out, you place the course for the start of a existence whole of pleasure and happiness. The first step is to roll up your sleeves and do something nice approximately the blockages.

You can be successful if you are happy which you deserve a higher existence and do the whole lot you could to gain this cause. But simply the decision isn't enough. You need to do some thing high quality about it.

Meet the annoying conditions

The route to a cutting-edge, better existence starts offevolved offevolved with a effective, energetic selection. This is which you dislike ache and do the whole thing viable to counteract it. On this terrific direction you may stumble upon small and additionally big traumatic conditions, pitfalls, headwinds and masses of different adversities. It is vital that you face and deal with them.

Some insights you gain inside the gadget are very painful. But the ache may be loads a great deal much less and ultimately dissolving into delight because of the truth you could address the present day-day understanding in a totally precise way. The small instructions will help you.

Important Info: The manual is thrilling for the ones humans who have issues with unique human beings and are searching out answers. It can't be used if demanding stories, together with abuse of any kind, have passed off. In the case of such research a therapist, physician or possibility practitioner have to be consulted to put off the blockage with their assist.

The Naikan approach for the right right here and now

To benefit self-records, the Naikan technique is a awesome approach to nice psychology. Translated from Japanese, "nai" approach interior and "kan" manner to take a look at. Accordingly, Naikan is not anything else than the immersion in a single's being. You discover yourself, learn how to look inner, understand and dissolve blockages.

There are 4 key questions that you can use to find out relationships with caregivers or precise issues. The specific function of the questions is which you do no longer appearance inwards from the mindset of the victim or offender. You take a independent characteristic. This offers you a modified, independent attitude on the elements which you are blocking off. With the subsequent four questions you could gather converting your existence.

They are perfect if you have issues in partnership, at artwork, in sexuality, with cash and other topics. You do now not have to expose your complete existence the other way up for this. Past matters belong to the past and most effective exist in the mind. That is why you start inside the proper proper here and now.

Life will cope with you and wrap blockages in educational items. Feel free to tear open the quite wrapping paper and spot what gift existence is imparting you with right now, even though it is able to occasionally give up painfully. The past is on the time table later. If you ever lose interest, you could technique the method of breaking apart the relationship together along side your parents. So, preserve that for later. First of all, it's miles approximately the "now", which want to have priority. The present is in which the lively existence takes area. Find a retreat wherein you can anticipate undisturbed. Look internal your self and look, for example, at a person, a state of affairs or activities that purpose you issues and pressure. This emotional stress creates terrible emotions. Take your pad and pencil with you in your island of rest and do not forget what this vital scenario seemed like. It is essential that you check the state of affairs or event neutrally and do no longer proper now fall over again into horrible feelings.

Light up the state of affairs or occasion with the following questions:

• What issues and troubles have I delivered about this character?

• What have I completed for this individual?

• What has this individual finished for me ultimately of this time?

• What did I study from the scenario? (Could I increase through the event?)

Write down everything that comes in your thoughts approximately the character or scenario. Chose sentences which includes:

• the man or woman (he/she) modified into disrespectful toward me

• I felt awful because of the fact...

• ...The character has given upward push...

• I am not accountable...

Then you'll be a victim fast. Strike those phrases out of your vocabulary. You're the nice who wants to make a cutting-edge, precise component of view.

But you can simplest try this if you test the opposite issue of the coin. Which problems have arisen for me via this individual, fall quick underneath the table because of the fact they seem beside the point inside the victim characteristic? How this query system works can be illustrated maximum without troubles with an instance.

Example:

You need to play soccer together with your offspring within the garden and the adjacent garage of the neighbor, which borders right now on your meadow, is ideally suited as a motive wall to shoot the balls in the direction of. Your neighbor dislikes this and starts to name you names. You straight away skip into competition, get angry and feature the right approach to hand. Your neighbor is so indignant that he threatens to call the police. Exactly At this 2nd you understand that the neighbor's aggression has also brought on aggression in you.

If you think about this case in greater detail and have a have a look at the questions once more, you may quick discover why the scenario ought to have escalated on this manner.

What problem did you purpose the neighbor?

Shooting balls in competition to the neighbor's garage wall irritated him. He became running focused inside the storage workshop and changed into continuously disturbed through the cause kicks. This disturbance creates stress, this is expressed in anger.

What did you do to your neighbor?

They took him significantly, listened to him, paid interest to him and his concerns and supplied treasured time.

What did your neighbor do for you in some unspecified time in the destiny of this time?

He sincerely needed to summon up masses of strength and braveness to deal with you. And he has sacrificed as a incredible deal time as you've got were given were given.

What did you studies from the scenario and the way might also want to you increase from this occasion?

One issue is plain! Your neighbor has created a scenario via his anger in which you advantage a deep perception into yourself. You speedy apprehend that you have aggression sound asleep indoors you which you do not need. This notion modifications your attitude. You can have a look at some component from every state of affairs and via every distinct character. No don't forget what the situation, there may be continually a excessive extremely good aspect, even in case you are deeply harm and upset in each different person.

Healing subjects from the beyond

They have damaged down the modern-day-day blockades. Nevertheless, there are even though barriers that stand within the manner of a happy, content fabric material lifestyles. Now is the time to have a look at the past and to take a better take a look at it.

Two versions are to be had because of this:

• Variant 1: You pass lower returned in your starting and have a look at your complete life so far.

• Variant 2: You select out up a demanding scenario or event that spontaneously involves mind.

With the number one opportunity, you will without a doubt now not don't forget the entirety that has befell to you on your life to date. Because the memory among 0 and 6 years is hidden in lots of elements at the back of opaque veils. Only a nice element may be resultseasily recalled. Do no longer decorate the facts and do no longer miss any elements. Use handiest the respective recollections that the thoughts gives you with at that second. As a primary step, take a look at the relationship you had in conjunction with your mother. Were you breastfed as an toddler, had been you bathed thru her and did she trade your diapers for you? As an little one, you have been a helpless creature relying at the mom's care.

Your mom supplied hundreds extra than requirements. For nights on give up she sat at your bedside or carried you at some stage in the residence because of the reality you have been crying or ill. She did many things that will help you broaden and become the individual you're these days.

When analyzing your existence to this point, you ought to cope with the high-quality things and situations. You make certain that the terrible topics get smaller and smaller. Try to pay interest at the quality matters for at the least 21 days. During this time you can gain some of statistics approximately your caregiver, can permit pass and sense freer. Mistakes that the caregiver has made grow to be much less tough to forgive. The ensuing blockages gradually dissolve till they have got disappeared truely. Get a notebook in which you may write down the whole thing in a quiet hour. Write down positive age intervals in order that your notes stay achievable.

This permits you to set the length from

• zero to 6 years

• 7 to twelve

• thirteen to 18

• Select 19 to 24 years.

During the number one week, write down everything that comes for your mind about the four questions concerning your mom. In the second one week you recognition in your father and start the cycle all over again.

The 2nd variant is used for demanding conditions within the gift and is achieved to sports that came about a hint at the identical time as within the past. Even if it's miles a large project, you want to try and recall the records. If you can't recall the statistics precisely, attempt to talk to the person who created the disturbing state of affairs. Through this form of verbal exchange many misunderstandings can be resolved and poor feelings eliminated.

Do no longer be dissatisfied if the alternative man or woman refuses your request for a communique. This is perfectly quality and should not inconvenience you. Always maintain in mind that now not everybody is willing to cooperate. Perhaps the "no" will offer you with the impetus to ask the 4 questions once more to benefit a present day angle on subjects. Integrate the questions as an essential part of your normal lifestyles. You may be surprised because of the fact you could activate the self-recuperation powers of the soul.

Learning to anticipate definitely

Positive wondering approach nothing other than seeing the exceptional components of each state of affairs and not letting horrific mind upward push up inside the first region. Positive wondering goes together with self-self belief. Confidence in your self lets in you to don't forget to your successes, the possibilities and offers you the electricity to the touch subjects that others don't forget unfeasible. Just test all the splendid successes in history. Behind they all is constantly excellent thinking! There emerge as one man or woman who believed in a unique opportunity and completed it. Positive questioning offers you with many benefits:

• You recognition on appropriate subjects that make you satisfied.

• Bad matters, failures and dangers make you prevent transferring earlier. Positive matters, however, deliver new impetus to get up and skip on. You stay capable of appearing.

• Positive questioning keeps frame and mind healthful.

• It boosts yourself-healing powers so you can defeat even the worst ailments.

• Positive thinking and the optimism that goes with it are the first rate situations for success within the professional and private vicinity.

• Positive wondering holds a pleasing lesson for you. You have the reins to your palms and can have an impact on your mind to a brilliant quantity. This way that you have clearly new and undreamt-of possibilities at your disposal.

• A satisfactory view of yourself and your successes strengthens your arrogance and self-self perception.

• You are open for brand new things and as a result growth your horizon.

• Your sensory organs and your notion characteristic an lousy lot higher via a super way of wondering. With this you're ready to interrupt new floor and not to close your eyes to it.

Many humans roll their eyes while the situation of "pleasant thinking" is addressed. The purpose for that may be a completely incorrect assumption approximately what powerful thinking way the least bit. They consider that when you expect really, terrible topics are without a doubt blanked out. This is incorrect! It is simply as wrong that super thinking people are dreamers. Optimism is as real as pessimism. There is nothing on this worldwide that is most effective first-rate. But it's far crucial to understand that even terrible subjects have a super component. You determine for yourself on which component you want to pay attention.

12 methods to sooner or later anticipate surely

1.) Do not be aware about terrible mind anymore!

As , horrible mind have terrific energy and are destructive. They have an effect on your temper, delight and braveness and make you experience lousy. Negative thoughts aren't really worth paying plenty interest to. This manner you could no longer wander off, but you may accumulate a totally actually one among a type weighting. If you another time quit that self-reproach, fears and problems are spreading or that simplest horrible thoughts are in the foreground, pull the ripcord very energetically and cope with other, effective topics that distract you from the horrible mind.

2.) Smile!

Again and again you meet people who undergo life with striking mouth corners and grouchy and all once more others who meet life with a grin on their face.

The humans with a grin on their lips are the happier ones. Researchers have determined out that a powerful facial abilities already releases happiness hormones. The mind absorbs the first rate facts transmitted thru the facial muscle groups. Smiling makes you happier and in addition cushty and you no longer see topics in fact black, but in plenty of particular solar sunglasses of coloration.

three.) Look for the good things in the conditions that stand up!

Every medal has sides, similar to each scenario. That's why you may no matter the truth that get a few aspect perfect out of every terrible experience, in case you use the proper interpretation. See negative things as a task and as a reading impulse. If you can not discover a parking region proper inside the the front of your door, you may get excessively indignant and grumble about it or revel in a hint walk in the glowing air after paintings. It might not generally be smooth to benefit some thing top notch from huge, existential conditions. If you've got honestly suffered a incredible loss, the recommendation "it'll probable be nicely for a few issue" may not be very beneficial.

However, when you have already appeared extra carefully at small matters and determined the notable aspect, you will be powerful however massive demanding situations.

four.) Write a diary of the belongings you are thankful for!

Not all topics are usually as terrible as they appear earlier than the whole lot. You are confident to come across many stuff for which you are grateful. You can write such topics for your gratitude diary. This manner you focus on the superb matters in place of paying too much interest to the terrible. Write down all the stuff you are grateful for in a unmarried quiet minute. It is not terrible in case you write down the same issue time and again once more, the important hassle is that you make yourself privy to it. With time, you may discover an increasing number of exquisite matters which you come upon in your lifestyles.

5.) Use a considered dosage of bad information!

No rely whether or not you switch at the TV and radio or browse social networks. Everywhere you look, you could find out disaster reports, so it is clean to get the have an effect on that there is now not anything superb in this international. Of path, there are violence and failures, but there also are at the least hundreds of thousands of tremendous topics. They truly do no longer display up at the statistics.

Just lower the flood of negative facts with the useful resource of not searching or paying attention to the statistics each hour and through the usage of most effective now and again surfing social networking web sites.

6.) Remove horrible humans out of your surroundings!

Whether your thoughts-set is immoderate remarkable or terrible is carefully related to the encompassing people. If you've got were given people round you all the time, who're great bitching and moaning, you brief adopt this attitude. It works the alternative manner spherical as nicely. If you surround your self with awesome humans, the outstanding mindset will rub off on you. So, look for the Sun Children and use exceptional psychology.

7.) Finally, climb out of the victim function!

Positively wondering humans additionally take full duty for their lives and do no longer blame one of a kind human beings. Therefore, you ought to say goodbye to the notion which you are the sufferer and most effective the horrible topics display up to you. You have superb have an effect on on your lifestyles. That's why you have to in no way permit pass of this crucial responsibility. You have the rudder for your hand and may determine wherein your supply is going.

Once you have got were given gained the statistics with all its outcomes, many opportunities and possibilities open up that permits you to take benefit of.

8.) Avoid comparing your self with others!

Why does the neighbor have a nicer house and a bigger car and why is the colleague extra a success than me? With those comparisons you create a nasty aftertaste that is assured to make you unwell for your stomach. You better take an first rate go searching. Some people are plenty worse off than you. Unfortunately this is finished an extended way too now not frequently. People almost continuously take a look at themselves with folks that are higher off. Stop it! If you manipulate to do that, your primary mind-set will robotically trade and superb thinking will take over.

9.) Use tremendous wondering on your achievement!

Even if you are not even privy to it, you have already finished such a whole lot of matters. Why no longer write down all of your successes, even the smallest ones? These encompass your college-leaving certificates, the studies you finished with a maintain near's diploma, your the usage of license, citing your kids, transferring to a larger, chic rental and recall the hard situations. There is assured to be masses of things involved. Add to the listing over and over with new successes, whether or not or no longer or no longer it's far the repaired tap or the education consultation inside the gym this is continuously dispose of. Write a every day list in which you enter your successes. It is notably more powerful than a to-do listing.

10.) Keep your dreams and your limits in mind!

Positive questioning is hard even as others are constantly trying to find to exceed your set limits. Show your limits and goals sincerely and continually maintain them in mind.

This essential step guarantees that you are accurate to yourself. This is the route of powerful psychology.

eleven.) After getting up, deal with fantastic thoughts!

If you begin the day with excellent thoughts, the entirety may be masses less tough and now not whatever can throw you off tracks. For you to achieve success, you need to bear in thoughts a situation early inside the morning in which you had been properly, in which you had been glad and glad.

Try to create the identical feelings as you probably did then and enjoy this first-rate 2nd to the complete.

12.) Read books that deal with the difficulty "Happiness" and "Being Happy"!

The situation be counted of "extraordinary wondering" and "being satisfied" covers plenty more than the elements listed. Therefore, you need to address the subject very intensively. With the correct literature you can have right helpers that will help you reconsider. Search for suitable literature within the book shop or on line. You will see that truly anyone who desires to may be satisfied.

Fears: an extended way-accomplishing outcomes on a glad existence

Fears aren't only burdensome. They have a far-accomplishing impact to your development, restriction and prevent you from taking factor on your existence simply. They are available superb forms. Experts agree that, depending on the diploma of hysteria, the extraordinary of existence is so extensively constrained that humans can perish from these horrible feelings. Their subdivision of tension every now and then looks as if this:

1. At the top of the list is fear, in which the sensation is described as hazard or chance. It is used to maintain off damage and to avoid conditions in order that the ones feelings of worry do not get up in the first place.

2. A heightened shape is everyday worry, which manifests itself in a threatening feeling that takes area at normal intervals while situations need to get out of hand.

3. The existential fear is part of life and consists of the concern of loneliness, lack of lifestyles,

curtailment of freedoms that eliminate yourself-willpower.

4. In the case of neurotic tension, as an example, the concern of rejection arises.

It is seen as a transition to a pathological form of fear. Sigmund Freud's definition of this fear is that guy is frightened of a danger he has now not yet skilled.

five. A phobia is a form of anxiety in which concrete subjects and situations motive the concern. This may be a confined area like an elevator, a spider, an examination or worry of social failure.

6. Obsessive wondering, conduct and movement is referred to as obsessive-compulsive fear. This includes, as an instance, the compulsion to easy, compulsive order or the compulsion to cleanliness.

7. Situations that can't be psychologically processed or prevented reason annoying fears.

These include natural failures, accidents, big violence and unexpected, immoderate infection.

These tension states can get up time and again, even a long term later. Experts call this "flashback".

8. Generalized fears accompany the affected character 24 hours a day. They awaken within the morning with those feelings and go to mattress with them within the night time. There isn't always any identifiable cause for those anxiety states or a whole collection of triggers, in order that worry is permanently gift.

9. Panic assaults seem . On the only hand, there is a concrete reason for them and but, they might arise absolutely unprepared. They are primarily based on a highbrow and physical response and generally do no longer ultimate longer than a few minutes.

10. Fears, coupled with a personality sickness, are based mostly on the concern of losing the ego, the self and identity. This outcomes in a lack of stability.

These ten sorts of worry are only a few fears that accompany people through life. To be able to do something positive about these fears, you should first find out what they may be based totally totally on.

Is this the primal fear that everybody has? It is innate and forestalls you from doing topics to be able to extraordinary harm you. The primal worry is managed by the use of intuition. It is, as an example, the priority of pain or loss of life and guarantees survival. Or is it fictitious fear this is handiest a pure creativeness? Your fantasy suggests you horrible snap shots in specific conditions, which may be spreading to your thoughts. They have no connection with reality and are exactly the opposite of the primal fear, it genuinely is quite justified. If your fears are fictional, there are numerous things you could do your self to manipulate them. Because the horror scenarios best manifest to your head and do now not need to stand up in actual lifestyles. Your mind create terrible pics and emotions of fear.

Imagine super pix of the occasion or state of affairs and the priority will no longer take you over. There are remarkable strategies to combat fictional tension and make sure that the emotions of anxiety disappear.

7 techniques to fight fear

For you to reach stopping your fears, the 7 strategies begin in which fear arises, especially for your head.

1.) Do the fact test to counter your fear!

On closer inspection, most fears are clearly exaggerated if you take a better take a look at them in the course of a reality test. You will rapid notice that during truth not whatever bad is because of it. You can do the Reality Check resultseasily through asking yourself whether or not or no longer or no longer the situation is clearly dangerous and what the worst issue which can show up to you is. The following examples display that your fears are unfounded:

worry of creating a mistake: Making a mistake is human. Besides, it commonly is based upon getting ready to view. If you have got were given made a mistake, you may usually correct it again. ?

Fear of alternate: Change does not mean hazard, but as an alternative possibilities to upward push above oneself. Through alternate, you make bigger yourself further and expand your horizon. ?

Fear of latest matters: You can fine amplify similarly if you strive new subjects. Even if the concern feels very real, you do now not recognise what to anticipate beforehand. If you seize the possibility, you could discover afterwards that your fears had been without a doubt incorrect. That's why you have to try new topics. ?

Fear of showing boundaries: Calmly show your counterpart limits he need to now not circulate and don't be afraid of them. The distinctive man or woman will neither attack you nor harm you and could fast understand that she or he has behaved improperly. ?

Fear of displaying the proper character: Nothing horrible will show up, confident, in case you display your real personality, your right self. Every person is individual and does not want to cover for this. People who do not like their actual self do no longer belong for your environment. ?

Fear of drawing close to extraordinary human beings: The handiest detail that could take location to you is rejection. Being rejected is not a notable feeling, however it suggests you right away that these humans have little recognize. You do not want such people. Make it clean to yourself that although it is an unpleasant feeling, it's going to no longer motive you similarly harm. ?

Fear of failure: Failure and screw ups are not some factor with a view to cause you physical harm. See defeats as a undertaking to develop and come to be higher. They open up new perspectives for you. So rise up all over again and start from scratch. ?

Fear of being on my own: Even though it feels terrible, you do now not must be fearful of being by myself. Make your self aware that being on my own being a pride due to the truth you sooner or later have time for your self, to meet your dreams and to reorder your life. ?

Fear what others don't forget you: This worry isn't always only unjustified, however surely senseless. You should now not care. Besides, maximum people have sufficient to do with themselves and are confident not to consider you. ?

Fear of public appearances, shows and challenge interviews: ?

The worst component which could take area to you are booing, shaking your head or possibly being pelted with rotten eggs. Try to be convincing and create great pics to your head. The fear is most effective based totally on fictitious fears that can be stimulated.

These are just a few matters that revel in uncomfortable. You create those emotions yourself on your head, however they do not cause you to revel in real pain or be in risk.

As quickly as you ask yourself what ought to seem to you in the worst case, you could find that the pix on your head do not correspond to reality in any respect. Once you recognise this, the fears lose their powerful effect.

2.) Change the pics in your head!

In addition to the reality test, you can without a doubt alternate the photographs in your head. The notion which you do no longer have an effect in your thoughts is wrong. If you want to, you can manage your thoughts.

Imagine a colorful flower meadow. Bet that you can see it right now in the the front of your internal eye!

All you want is the eye which you are accountable for your mind. As quick as fear units in, you need to consciously recognize the pictures to your head and appearance intently at what they display. If they spread fear, attempt to erase them. You can do that via way of creating the image small or vague, tearing it up or portray over it with vibrant colours. If you preserve seeking to do this, it'll probable be easy for you. Try to update the horrible pix with excessive top notch ones. You can try this with the aid of imagining the apparently negative image inside the most adorable shades. Through your imagination you create a incredible notion to your mind and therefore replace the terrible thoughts. Mental pics are the notable mystery weapon in the course of fears.

three.) Learn to manipulate your thoughts!

The extra aware you are of your thoughts, the much less hard it is for you to influence them. A extremely good technique for greater interest of your mind is meditation. With meditation, you can get off the merry-cross-round of your thoughts and definitely allow skip of awful feelings. It offers peace and greater interest. You do no longer need to meditate for hours for this. A little while an afternoon is sufficient.

In addition to highbrow peace and relaxation, meditation additionally creates a extraordinary feeling within the body, which also has a extremely good impact on emotions of fear.

Info: If you're free and comfortable, you can not enjoy worry simultaneously!

four.) Use achievement inside the direction of fear as a secret weapon!

Feelings of success are a exceptional way to fight fears. Each time you've got triumph over fear, you can have fewer horrific feelings the following time. You revel in that no longer something lousy can seem and broaden a modern day self-self perception. Do this little by little earlier than you face the massive fears. To attain stopping worry, you may endure in thoughts tales of fulfillment. Remember situations in which you've got faced and conquer your fear. These do now not need to be large matters. Even the small topics have a massive impact. The reality on my own makes you experience correct because you have got were given fought the priority of a remarkable event your self. By remembering such conditions over and over, you take place them to your unconscious:

"I can try this, irrespective of what happens!" With this you will acquire that there may be nothing greater to be terrified of.

five.) Face your fears together!

Sometimes fears make bigger if you have to stand them on my own. For instance, you can discover it a good buy worse when you have to talk on my own in the front of an target marketplace or on the same time as you skip domestic by myself in the dark than even as you are with other humans. A employer offers you a stable feeling and manual. This makes you experience drastically more potent yourself. Find humans on your surroundings who are not afraid of situations or topics that scare you. In the identical way, you may surround your self with human beings who've already conquer fears. They show you that you could face your fears without some component horrible taking region.

6.) Counteract your horrific thoughts with the useful resource of acting!

The extra you bear in mind a state of affairs, event or factor, the more worry builds up. This is pretty logical, as you spend an entire lot of energy on imagining bad photographs to your mind. Be faster than your thoughts and get inside the fast lane so as not to conjure up the worst conditions to any extent further.

This does no longer imply which you are speeding into threat. Keep the time of thought to a minimum and ask yourself if the hassle or situation is threatening. Then you have to do it! Speak to the fascinating female or the exquisite man subsequent to you on the bar, at the same time as no longer having to go through 1,000 versions to your head.

There is not any proper or wrong. The only factor that can seem is which you get a rejection! Go on stage in a karaoke bar and hold close the microphone earlier than terrible thoughts upward thrust up approximately how the target market might probable react. By appearing right away and being brave, you may banish terrible mind and horror scenarios out of your thoughts.

7.) Let the ache of terrible feelings take impact!

Of direction fears aren't excellent feelings. But what opportunity is there to counteract them. Fear has you firmly in its grip and stops you from growing above yourself and breaking new ground. Try to stand your fear and permit the pain come. You can do this by means of manner of way of imagining your life in advance than your inner eye in case you do not face your fear and fight it.

Try to sense the sensations that arise. Think about it,

• what you are missing out on due to your fears,

• what evaluations you may bypass over

• and what policies on the best of existence the fears supply with them.

Those are not pretty performances!

Now consider how glad and fulfilled your life is probably if you have triumph over your fears. Create pics of the manner lots greater fun you could have in lifestyles at the same time as the fears are lengthy past. Without fear, you can in the long run formulate new goals and understand them. In you is the capability to subsequently begin a satisfied, contented life.

Learning to recognize your self and the use of this information for personal development

There are the ones well-known, easy statements that make you watched and provoke dissatisfaction. One such statement is:

"Before I can exchange, I need to first understand myself!"

But what does it endorse to understand oneself? If you are sincere now, you can speedy comprehend that your way of questioning and acting can be very difficult. You can hopefully surrender the declare to apprehend yourself. But for the duration of your life you may constantly studies some issue approximately yourself and as a result have the opportunity to change something. It is splendid that human beings are capable of exchange, even though they expect they do not recognize themselves the least bit and do not recognize their moves.

As confusing as this will sound, human beings can trade because of the truth they replicate on their way of wondering and performing and find out that they advantage some attention. There is readability which deepens the very own self-image. Self-statistics arises, for example, through other folks that offer feedback on their character, behavior or expressions.

This does now not advise criticism, however as an alternative the concrete observations that one in all a type people make whilst managing you. However, your effect on special human beings is great one point amongst many others. It is likewise vital whether or not the photo of others and your photograph of yourself pass collectively and whether or not or not you reach conveying your perspectives efficiently.

To increase self-photograph, you need to reply the subsequent questions:

• Who am I?

• What form of person am I?

• Why am I like this and now not specific?

• What can turn out to be of me?

One of the maximum hard questions in terms of content material material and approach is that of "why".

This often shows communication patterns that you were faced with in your existence and although are. There are special patterns that are not very useful for self-discovery.

These include questions inclusive of "Why are you doing this over again?" or "How have to you have got...? Such questions embarrass and misery you.

Let's move lower back to the proper question. If you want to alternate some thing, you could trade a few detail even without a concrete purpose. Something better can give up result from such an strive. However, the efforts can be more powerful in case you apprehend the concrete connections. You can obtain this with a behavioral assessment. Many human beings assume that this is very confined however on closer exam, it will become smooth that the questions on the "why" are not first-class superficial however flow into intensity. In doing so, you may benefit a comprehensible rationalization and statistics for some conduct, that allows you to offer a boost to this conduct. Sometimes other human beings are the reinforcers who react on your conduct. That is why some people make pretty a few nonsense honestly to get noticed and applauded.

Self-information moreover manner that you get to the bottom of the query which mechanisms are chargeable for your conduct. If evidently behavior patterns are only used to attract interest, you've got a tangible way of changing your conduct.

If you spot yourself as someone who orientates himself towards others and does matters which do not correspond for your thoughts, you have to gain perception and receive this orientation. Ask yourself the questions whether or not or not or now not what you do makes enjoy and whether you want to do it.

Understanding oneself, consequently, approach not anything greater than coping with one's tendencies and perspectives and developing readability. With this clarity you get a view of factors and might determine whether to alternate or hold your existence software program. If making a decision to be incredible, you return lots closer to yourself and get to understand yourself a touch higher once more. That is why you need to get rid of stuff you do not want out of your life and best do the things you need! Ask yourself time and again whether or not you need to do this and what you truly love!

In this way you lay the foundation for developing a higher statistics of your self and expanding your personality. In addition to self-information and data yourself better, you moreover may additionally want a high quality diploma of information of human nature to benefit a higher facts and appreciation of others.

Gaining statistics of human nature and the usage of it to obtain one's non-public desires

Knowledge of human nature is likewise an thrilling subject matter in immoderate first rate psychology. Because emotionally practical humans see the sector with sincerely precise eyes. They can understand, have an effect on and apprehend the feelings of others. People with emotional intelligence are real leaders due to the fact they're able to manipulate their emotions and the emotions of others to obtain desires.

In regularly, we consider that one appearance is sufficient so that you can check a few different man or woman. However, to apprehend how the opposite character honestly ticks, a higher appearance is vital. Because first impressions can be deceptive. The first look is best a spontaneous assessment made from the prevailing moment. This suggests handiest a small segment. You simplest look inside the decrease back of the façade when you have proper statistics of human nature.

Great temptation and lurking risks

The exquisite temptation is to look any other individual in the attention and have the ability to tell at once what makes that man or woman tick. It is tempting to be able to inform with without a doubt one look whether the opposite character is glad, sad or worrying and what makes up their person. Unfortunately, this isn't always feasible so in reality. Reading faces is a lesson that has involved people for the reason that historical instances. Among the oldest data are writings with the aid of Aristotle, who treated this problem.

The assumption effects within the reality that highbrow trends are quick deduced from a person's appearance in a fragment of a 2d. The brief shot ends in a misjudgment and rapidly stirs up prejudices. That is why actual know-how of human nature and now not absolutely 1/2 of-know-how is needed! In the past, so-called physiognomy come to be considered an art work and mystery expertise. It have become particularly utilized by clergymen for occult functions. In later eras, even as the Enlightenment become at the leading edge, this branch of expressive psychology became greater important and come to be an increasing number of identified as a scientific education.

Unfortunately, the modern findings in physiognomy, which got here to slight through generation, delivered about terrible outcomes. They were no longer used to position oneself in distinctive people's shoes higher, to cultivate a greater sensitive approach and to fulfill variations with appreciation. Rather, it have come to be used within the nineteenth and twentieth centuries to underpin racism and eugenics on a systematic degree.

First indication of information of human nature

The form of the pinnacle, the width of the mouth or the height of the brow are said to indicate trends inclusive of power of will and intelligence. This assumption remains causing loads of dialogue in social psychology due to the fact specialists remember that it does no longer lead to a higher information of different people. Numerous studies additionally come to one in all a kind conclusions.

However, there can be one component on which the experts agree: The first judgment you are making approximately another character is superficial. But it may be used to provide a tough outline of the alternative character's character. This first judgment you're making about any other individual can be a protecting mechanism derived from evolution. Before you permit every different individual get inside the route of you, try to defend yourself. You observe him/her extra intently and decide intuitively due to the number one have an effect on whether or not the man or woman method nicely with you or is to be seen as an enemy. While this initial evaluation is beneficial, it is awesome a number one indication based definitely absolutely to your emotions and assessment.

Reading emotions within the face of the other individual

To higher check out extraordinary human beings, the US psychologist Paul Ekman has evolved a method known as Facial Action Coding System (FACS).

It dates again to 1978 and permits you to turn out to be privy to seven simple emotions from the muscle movements on your face. According to the psychologist, they may be located in every person. These embody fear, anger, surprise, disgust, disappointment, satisfaction and contempt. Today, many laptop applications for emotion reputation are primarily based mostly on the FACS approach. However, the approach is as a substitute controversial, because it does not recall that facial expressions can be managed. That is why critics assume that there may be no manner to make a accurate assessment with it.

Taking your have an impact on into account

If you want to evaluate each different person efficiently, you need to be conscious that this doesn't work within the beginning look due to the fact you aren't able to looking on the opportunity person neutrally.

Your evaluation is based on what you word and on your self or your mood, your studies and cultural background. People rashly positioned unique people proper right into a certain drawer, even though they however lack a whole lot of data that justifies this sorting. Always undergo in mind that the outward appearance does no longer provide a view of internal values. To understand the ones, you want to appearance more carefully and ask questions.

How does the individual deal with exceptional people? What are his beliefs? What is critical for him?

Proceed with care

Especially in terms of topics that seem vital to you, you must exercise care and no longer make a hasty evaluation or judgement. Even if you suppose you have got correct knowledge of human nature, you will be absolutely wrong alongside side your assessment. You do no longer have an effect on the number one, spontaneous have an effect on. However, you may use the primary affect to take some different nearer look and in all likelihood revise your first opinion. This is a sincere change. It can even be a great asset to you. At 2nd look, humans who've judged you hastily may moreover come to be excellent, treasured human beings.

5 recommendations to decorate your judgement

1. Remain open and alert, and continuously do not forget that you in no way observe others

objectively. Your approach is primarily based completely in your revel in.

2. Appearances aren't any indication of someone's person. Attractive does not suggest that this man or woman is also clever, fats does no longer suggest that the character is humorous. These are just clichés into which humans need to brief classify one among a type humans.

3. Question your prejudices. Because pretty unconsciously you decide humans or age companies even as no longer having contemplated on them because of the fact your manner of questioning is common through prejudices.

4. Train empathy. Before you provide a horrible assessment approximately each one of a kind individual, you want to try and placed your self of their area.

Why does this person react like that? What is in the again of it? What is the cause for his movement?

5. Also concentrate for overtones in the conversation. They show hundreds about the opportunity individual. That's why you need to pay interest cautiously and apprehend how the alternative character says a few problem. This will will let you recognise masses about the man or woman.

Manipulation: Covert have an impact on on thinking and acting

Are you privy to the situation that you abruptly specific critiques, utter utterances and effective techniques of wondering appear, which occasionally do now not correspond to your normal wondering and performing in any manner and are opposite to your nature? Then you have got have been given met a person who's a hold close of manipulation. You stumble upon manipulative humans anywhere and also you do not also be aware that thoughts and evaluations are implanted for your head. You have emerge as a puppet of your associate, buddies, paintings colleagues or a speaker who inspired your manner of thinking and performing with outstanding persuasive energy.

Manipulation consists of the Latin terms "manus" (hand) and "plere" (fill) and has the meaning of "coping with". The meaning within the enjoy of "handling" is still used in recent times. In sociology, politics and psychology, manipulation is known to intend the concealed exertion of impact.

Those who control different humans use a complicated technique, concealing the actual motives, which might be frequently self-hobby, to gain a bonus and reap a fine intention. Manipulative behavior does now not always need to be observed via a disruption. However, if it's far intense, it may be an delinquent person illness, on the aspect of narcissism. If one among a kind humans are used as a device to use manipulative, misleading conduct for their benefit, the arrival of the illness counts as a psychopathic ailment.

Influence is the often used synonym for manipulation. However, the problem of focused exploitation is lacking. Politics, as an instance, uses influencing to persuade the population of their perspectives and actions and to disseminate ideological mind. Political have an effect on is likewise referred to as propaganda. If you cross decrease lower back in modern-day history, you'll find out a daunting example in Nazi propaganda. Emotional influencing of various people for one's profits in no manner corresponds to the easy idea that everyone has for himself. Everyone desires to make alternatives autonomously and freely, based on their passion and purpose. They ought to not be the end end result of manipulation.

9 Signs of manipulation

Many factors permit you to decide whether or now not or no longer your counterpart is attempting to control you. The highbrow manipulation manifests itself in the following behaviors, among others. You do now not get an answer and your conversation companion accommodations to sarcasm. You are counseled that it isn't feasible to talk to you or you're spoken to as when you have been a infant. Your interviewer offers you an ultimatum.

Especially in verbal exchange and language many sorts of mental manipulation are hidden. By using them, humans pass at the path of emotional abuse and intellectual exploitation. Some people master the abuse of language flawlessly and may manipulate, manual and direct humans. This was furthermore examined via the neo-fascist Licio Gelli within the data of Italy, who specialised in manipulating big hundreds of humans. Accordingly, you best need to understand how to talk well to gain manage over one-of-a-type people.

Quote:

"Thoughts corrupt what's said, and what's said can corrupt human relationships."

George Orwell

Everyone is aware of such ordinary situations only too well. Because you're exposed to normal manipulation in lots of areas, whether or not or not in politics, the media or via extraordinary advertising ensures. A purpose is thereby to persuade you to your choice to seduce and manage. Significantly extra flexible and fuller of secrets and techniques and strategies and strategies is the manipulation, which takes location inside the private area.

In communication together with your accomplice, pals and different family individuals it has an ideal, mature camouflage, so that the lure snaps close unexpectedly, or you operate it your self. It is consequently important that you appearance cautiously at what you are saying and cope with manipulative statements with care. Therefore, pay near interest to the selection of your sentences. In desired, you want to understand the manner to stumble on mental have an effect on and react to it successfully.

Recognizable skills of highbrow impact

If verbal intellectual manipulation takes region, there may be an imbalance inside the dating amongst you and your interlocutor. The other person desires to gain a private gain through language, manipulate you or maybe damage you. The resulting emotions generate hidden aggression no longer best in the unique man or woman, but also in your self, which makes all signs to attack. Words have the exceptional power to penetrate the whole thing and do not even save you on the identification, self-esteem or dignity of the opportunity individual. To assist you recognize intellectual manipulation, you can now discover how to reveal it.

1. Facts get twisted!

Manipulative human beings who have perfect mastery of intellectual have an impact on are specific strategists and have first-rate mastery of twisting the reality in their need.

In doing so, they location the primary blame at the shoulders of the interlocutor and reduce his percent of responsibility. Important records do now not come to the desk the least bit or are exaggerated. The adjustment is made to this form of immoderate degree that it corresponds precisely to at least one's notion of the truth.

2. Accusing that it is now not possible to talk to you!

Behind this announcement isn't always handiest directness but additionally effectiveness due to the fact the interlocutor refuses to speak approximately a hassle. You are accused of being some distance too emotional and of creating a huge deal out of a hint issue. With such statements you're blamed, even though the alternative character is the accountable birthday party. This is evidence of a lack of communication talents.

3. Bullying at an intellectual degree

Manipulators also like to apply verbal exchange techniques which may be on an intellectual degree. You are continuously bombarded with all forms of statistics, arguments, twisted common revel in and data, that have exceptional one goal: to emotionally exhaust you till you're glad that your interlocutor is proper.

four. Set an ultimatum with a respectable time-body

Statements at the side of "You have till day after today to think about it" and "If you do now not need to absolutely be given what has been stated, this is the cease of it" have in all likelihood already been said to you. Such comments are incriminating and hurtful. You will fast locate yourself in a capture 22 scenario that brings emotional struggling and worry. Always recollect that someone who clearly loves and respects you can never count on an all-or-nothing preference from you. People you try to manipulate in this manner do not belong for your immediate environment due to the fact they best damage you.

five. Repeat the call of the person opposite you continuously in verbal exchange!

The steady, non-stop and exaggerated repetition of your call in verbal exchange is a sign of a clever manipulate mechanism. This is supposed to ensure that you concentrate attentively and are higher able to intimidate.

6. Humiliation with black humor and irony!

Your interlocutor mocks you thru injecting black humor and ironic comments into the verbal exchange. This kind of intellectual manipulation serves to belittle you, undermine you and play on his superiority. In specific words, the aggressor tells you that you are not equal to him and therefore you cannot have your opinion.

7. Feigning lack of awareness

A traditional for feigned lack of awareness is the sentence: "I do now not know what this is all about!" Your communique associate pretends to be stupid and pretends to have no concept what it's far all approximately and what you need to gather with the verbal exchange. Attention! This is where your thoughts is being performed with. You are faced with the accusation which you most effective complicate topics and that a conversation is certainly pointless. This technique is regularly utilized by aggressors to make you undergo and now not to take duty.

8. Your verbal exchange accomplice offers you the right of way within the communicate!

Even if this intellectual manipulation is diffused, the strategy has a specially massive effect. Because the interlocutor achieves two subjects with it. Firstly, he has won sufficient time to react for your statements and arguments and inside the intervening time he can choose out inclined factors to strike this notch. Sometimes, however, the manipulator moreover refrains from expressing his opinion and thoughts.

Questions are really requested, and shortcomings are searched for, as opposed to finding a high-quality commonplace solution. By this way of manipulation the interlocutor succeeds in making you sense like a inclined, clumsy character. Psychological and emotional manipulation has many more, sudden aspects.

But the indexed ones belong to the common strategies you could come upon time and again. They are used to intimidating and for that reason prevent a huge alternate in communique.

The techniques located you out of motion on a intellectual, non-public and emotional degree. It is consequently of huge importance that manipulative techniques are diagnosed and that they are resisted.

Ways of protection in opposition to covert manipulation

Dubious procurement of statistics

If your interlocutor tries to sound you out and the conversation resembles an interview, the communication targets at amassing facts. At first, the have an effect on might also stand up that this person desires to recognize extra approximately you. This is mostly a correct element, if the ulterior motive isn't always to use the data to govern you. For manipulation to be successful, your susceptible factors should be recognized. The manipulator will in no way display his weaknesses and could excellent display you his strengths. Be cautious what you assert. The aggressor will take gain of your weaknesses. He does not care if it harms you.

Defense desire: Avoid that the communique is satisfactory one-manner and display the interlocutor that you have in reality as masses proper to understand some element about her or him.

A a achievement communique is not a questioning activity, however conversation primarily based on mutuality. Only inform as a bargain approximately yourself as you want to expose.

Resist the persuasions that nook you and tempt you to reveal more facts. Ask the interviewer and counter his questions with counter-questions. This manner the manipulator brief realizes that he can not intimidate you and you defuse the situation.

False truths

Manipulative human beings often tell stories that by no means befell and attempt to give you information that is truly incorrect. Unfortunately, this isn't recognized proper away. Manipulators do honor to the lie baron von Munchhausen and do not even have a horrible moral experience. To unmask such a person, you want to take a close to check the cause of the facts and data. A liar now and again exposes himself due to the reality he solutions unimportant questions excessively, justifies and explains. When situations stand up that denounce the liar and query his or her honesty, she or he will be able to need to justify himself or herself verbosely so that she or he isn't always positioned inside the wrong light.

Defensive desire: If you consider you studied you have got a manipulative man or woman within the front of you, you can divulge it fast. If a declaration appears dubious to you, take the opportunity to invite questions. If the interviewer will become aggravating and evades your questions, you could almost expect that the tale is not actual.

Targeted take a look at-up and questioning motives the manipulative individual to get out of the street of hearth.

Exaggerated attraction

One of the quality guns of manipulation is appeal. If you stumble upon a person who pays you charming compliments, you can almost really count on that your verbal exchange partner is a manipulator. Take a near look to look if there may be some component else in the again of the attraction or if this man or woman is truly charming in the direction of special human beings.

Selfishness hides within the lower lower back of enchantment even as

• You receive compliments earlier than a request is made,

• the character is handiest there for you in such conditions if he/she enjoys blessings from them,

• would love the gesture to present him a bonus,

• the attraction is first-class applied in high-quality situations and

• very little appeal is applied in specific situations.

If those factors comply with to your interlocutor, she or he has most effective selfish reasons, which she or he desires to put into effect with captivating behavior.

Defense: Don't be blinded with the useful resource of the charming behavior of your verbal exchange companion however have a observe his conduct and question why he's so fascinating right now. Charm have to not be entangled with situations or conditions. If the person you are talking to is charming, you do not want to look this as an obligation. You can say "no" if he comes at some point of the nook with a select or a request after a fascinating offensive. Prevent that your real nature is exploited and that the manipulator receives the whole thing from you through his attraction.

A nearer test function patterns

People who need to take advantage of you often appear as martyrs. They present themselves as accurate-natured, self-sacrificing and helping human beings. Such males and females appear sympathetic and accumulate all compassion. In this manner they have opened all doorways to manipulate you. The aggressor has quick recognized wherein your weaknesses lie and makes use of them for emotional blackmail. He has diagnosed what he can use to damage you and criticize you in a targeted way. In this manner he creates a feel of inferiority in you, which regularly outcomes in an emotional duty. You do the whole thing to pleasure this person.